Is Trump Treasonable?

Consider The Evidence

The Duty to Warn
As Seen By a Psychologist 7.0

Paschal Baute, Ed.D.

ISBN-13: 978-1545051719

ISBN-10: 1545051712

Parts of this book were previously
Published in *Shit Stirrer in the Oval Office*,
2017, Paschal Baute

Baute Publishing
4080 Lofgren Ct.
Lexington, Ky. 40509

An Explanation Of Our Logo.

Our logo suggests we humans have three selves or three voices: Child, Adult and Parent. The **Child** self is our total bodily experience: sensations and feelings. It is immediate, without reflection.

The **Adult** self is rational, logical reasoning. Here we sort, process the messiness and complexity sorting our reality objectively like a computer,

The **Parent** self is the source of our values, and rules, functioning as a road map or GPS system, here we judge our experience according to our chosen rules and values.

We are aware of these different inner selves as we face the ups and downs of life.

Our task in coping with stress and developing resilience is to learn to listen to all these voices. Our inner dialogue becomes a reflective guide to help us survive and thrive. Our aim is to help your reading become a thoughtful exercise evoking hope, courage and resilience.

Each chapter is an invitation to an inner dialogue, listening to your own GPS, "Recalculating," developing resilience, inch by inch. The logo reminds the reader that this a summoning to a thoughtful conversation with the ideas presented.

TABLE OF CONTENTS

Prologue: The Duty To Warn

The Duty to Warn in case of danger to others is an ethical imperative for psychologists. Dr. Paschal Baute, an Organizational Psychologist has screened thousands for every job level. He raises critical questions both before and after the 2016 presidential election concerning the job fitness of Donald Trump.

This is my sixth book on Trump, each about one hundred pages, each offering a variety p of not only perspectives of his behavior but a plethora of choices for resilience, serving and thriving, no matter what. These books are listed in the back matter of this book under "Other Books by the Author."

A psychologist has the duty to warn when he encounters a person who is dangerous to others health and well -being. This book aims to explain the threat to all of us. Although I listen to other psychologists and members of the mental Health professional community, I do to think it is helpful to offer a clinical diagnosis. I attempt to stay with observable behavior. Some behavior is so regular and consistent that implications can be drawn for wellbeing or not

"As far as ethics go, I would argue with my colleagues that those who don't speak out are being unethical. If we have knowledge and understanding about the unique danger that Donald Trump presents through our psychiatric training and we don't say something about it, history is not going to judge us kindly."- Rosemary Sword and Philip Zimbardo, PH.D., "The Elephant in the Room," *Psychology Today*, February 28, 2017. See also Lee Siegel, *Columbia Journalism Review* titled, "Avoiding Questions about Donald Trump's Mental Health Is a Betrayal to Public Trust."

Now some50 days plus into Donald Trump's presidency, urgent questions are: How Is Trump Managing as CEO of the U.S.A.? What Do We Do When The President Is a Liar? Is Donald Trump Mentally Unstable? Can Trump Affect Our Mental Health: American's Therapist Report? We answer these questions with substantial research.

On March 20, FBI Director Comey revealed an investigation into the Trump campaign over possible cooperation with Russian cyber attempts to influence our election. We include a time line of troublesome events outlined by Adam Schiff, (Rep. CA), minority chair of the House Select Committee on Intelligence. Representative Schiff laid out the evidence that demands a most serious investigation for the security and wellbeing of our nation.

Definitions

Terms defined. Treason, noun.

1. The offense of acting to overthrow one's government or to harm or kill its sovereign.

2. Violation of allegiance to one's sovereign or to one's state.

3. The betrayal of a trust or confidence; breach of faith; treachery.

Synonym Study

1.   Treason, sedition mean disloyalty or treachery to one's country or its government. Treason is any attempt to overthrow the government *or impair the well-being of a state to which one owes allegiance; the crime of giving aid or comfort to the enemies of one's government*. Sedition is any act, writing, speech, etc., directed unlawfully against state authority, the government, or constitution, or calculated to bring it into contempt or to incite others to hostility, ill will or disaffection; it does not amount to treason and therefore is not a capital offense..

Source: *Dictionary.com* Unabridged, Based on the Random House Dictionary, © Random House, Inc. 2017.

Example:

" 'When Dr. King said he was against the Vietnam War, he was accused of treason,' Jackson remembers."

Treasonable. adjective. Capable of, fitted for or likely to engage in treason

Examples:

"Trump's uncritical endorsement of Putin as an admirable leader while disparaging the leadership of President Obama is treasonable."

"I found a person who might spy for our country and with enough money he could be treasonable. '

Is Trump Treasonable?

Count the Red Flags – 21

Consider these questionable Trump behaviors *with* Russia and their cyber-war hacking:

1)   Trump has repeatedly praised the murderous dictator Putin.

2)   When the Russian hacking news was presented to him, he denied it, disparaged it, and called our loyal career professionals "Nazi." Only much later, months begrudging admitted it was true.

3)   Trump has never condemned this cyber-attack on our Nation's democratic process, an act of war, never spoken against it. This I find the most questionable behavior of all.

4)   Trump declared repeatedly that none of his campaign had any conversations with the Russians, now proven

repeatedly to be false, since seven have admitted conversation. Why the cover-up?

5)   When FBI Director Comey on March 20 in testimony, Trump actually and blatantly tweeted it was not true.

6)   Trump has not given any good faith, cooperation to the investigation,

7)   Evidence is clear the White House is controlling the House Committee designated to investigate the Russian influence, via is the suck up Committee Chair Nunes strange behavior.

8)   Trump cannot be counted on to tell the truth about anything. He lives in a fact-free self-chosen reality. He cannot admit any fault in anything.

9)   Trump has demonstrated to have no ethical rudder, no fixed principle, except his will to power and wealth, no scruples about heedless and shameless lying and numerous examples of "Bait and switch" with no intention to follow through on promises. e.g. "health care for all." (See my chapter in preparation on his numerous examples of bait and switch, broken promises and how he obtained such a cheering audience...)

10)   Trump publicly praised hacking of his opponent and declared he "loved" WikiLeaks, the Russian agent of email release.

11)   After learning his National Security Advisor Flynn had lied to VP Pence about speaking to the Russians Ambassador, he waited more than two weeks to fire him, doing so only after it became public news. Was this behavior Ad is denial not treasonable before it became public? Did Trump intend to cover up treasonable behavior of an accomplice? Flynn had been paid by Russians and by Turkey to be an agent even while he advised Trump all during the campaign. Was Flynn Trump's Russian Contact?

12)   Trump has declared all media except suck up Fox News to be the enemy of the people, pronouncing all critical news to be 'fake news. This arrogant claim undermines ether very rock principle of our democracy, and is characterized by would be

fascist dictators wanting complete control of opinion and people. Even more worrisome is the number of loyal followers are prepared to believe him.

13) Give #7 above with continued Shit Stirring and defensive behavior of the President, no independent investigation, at this time seems possible.

14) At the Republican convention the only item in the policy platform that the Trump party asked to be DELETED was ONLY ONE which stated we would offer weapons to Ukraine to defend themselves against the 'Russians.

15) After repeatedly saying he would release his taxes, Trump has refused even though most Americans toddy thinks he should. Records show he owes 3000 million to a Russian bank. Is this is only reason for hiding his taxes?

16) One thing we now know perfectly clear is that we cannot expect the white House to be truthful with any request. They can no more tell the truth than the President.

17) There is at least the "smell of treason" here as the New York Times said las t week.

18) If there is nothing to be found as the White House now insists (March 28, Sean Spicer), then the quickest way to put all these questions behind then is to appoint a special independent Prosecutor. Why will they not do this?

19) Either out of pure ignorance of the international order of allied democracies sustained by our United States for 72 years, or in cooperation with Putin's goals, Trump has tried to weaken NATO by praising the British Breckit, doubting the value of NATO and publicly haranguing NATO member nations re paying more for their mutual defense.

20) After promising repeatedly he would release his tax returns, Trump has refused, one of over 100broken promises catalogued by investigative reporters. It has been since verified he owes a Russian bank 300 million dollars. Is he not liable to blackmail or persuasion by a foreign power by that debt? His

refusal to release his taxes is not just suspicious but dangerous to our national security.

21) The March 30 testimony at the Senate committee investigating the Russian hacking, in response to the question of how they could be so successful, the stunning answer was: "The Russians were helped because both the candidate and his campaign AMPLIFIED, that is, helped the Russians. This fact itself makes this book worth the effort in the questions raised.

Therefore:

<u>We now know that Trump</u>

A) At least knew of campaign staff accepting and welcoming the
Russian hacking.

B) Further that Trump himself, with no known values except self-promotion and the will to power, likely approved the hacking and offered quid pro quo.

Trump is possibly guilty of treason against these Unlived States of America and is now trying desperately through surrogates to cover his tracks.

What other understanding can you offer to these many questionable behaviors?

Urgent: contact Speaker Paul Ryan today, to demand removal of Rep. Devin Nunes from position of Chair of House Intel committee investigating the Russian hacking. Nunes is obviously compromises in three ways, 1) making unilateral decisions without involving committee, 2) secretly advising the President about secret information, and unilaterally cancelling schedule work.

Without an independent investigation, we cannot know the answers. The White House is managing a cover up. Note: if Trump is treasonable, he is not our legitimate president

Now the House Intel Select Committee is now stalled by Devin Nunes, its Chair. We need investigation to continue both by our Senate and our House of Representatives. Call Speaker Ryan to demand Rep. Devin Nunes be removed from House Intel committee chair for obvious bias at @ 202-225-0600.

Trump's Will To Power

Never have we seen such a political candidate, now President, such as Donald Trump. Never in recent or more distant history, perhaps since the Civil War, have we had anyone who has so divided our country.

Donald Trump defies categories; he is "sui generis", meaning one of a kind. Whatever happens to his presidency, he will continue to fascinate, captivate, disgust, amuse or scare his audience, whenever, however. So strong is the bond he has created with his followers, one would dismiss all evidence of cooperation with the Russians even if proven by our FBI.

Trump has captivated and mesmerized a large part of our electorate. Such is his bond with many of his followers that he bragged he could shoot someone in broad daylight without legal harm. A relative in coal country in Eastern Kentucky was warning his co-worker that if Trump's budget went through, they would lose their jobs. She replied, "I don't care. I just love him."

The scary part of this infatuated loyalty is that a substantial number of our citizens are ready to believe every lie even those lies discredited by everyone else. And he knows it. On the other hand, Trump has scared, disgusted or terrified the other half. Trump never found a rule or social norm he was not ready to break; now including to everyone's surprise, every political norm. He has an immense capacity to seize headlines, to captivate, confound, please or and aggravate the public. So drenched in "Trumpism" are many, they have relinquished, with cognitive fatigue, paying any attention. When we give up caring about facts, about the truth, we have succumbed to an evil genius. This is why this book must be written by a blind veteran using training of the Hines VA Blind Rehab Center.

Trump has believed he is destined for great material wealth and world prominence. We examine briefly the main thrusts of Trump's behavior until now, when he is so out of his space that he knows he must fake it, realizing he is abysmally ignore of the real world order. As the FBI investigation of the possible cooperation of his campaign with Russian intelligence proceeds, he is likely to become more unstable.

Other than his will to power and wealth, Trump seems to have no fixed principle. A subtle but obvious paranoiac already infuses the White House: 1) All the press, except Fox News is the enemy; 2) He is the victim of wire-tapping no matter what anyone else says; 3) Sixteen "aides" have been appointed to each Cabinet Secretary to observe and report only to the White House. If you are not for "The Donald 100%, you must be against him. And you will pay, sooner or later!

Trump's will to power has worked so well, he creates his own reality, not needing facts, but only his feelings for his certainty. He has become a masterful in stirring trouble by creating stories to amuse, distract and promote his goals

Trump then discovered that the will to win could prevail even in chaos. In fact, he could even create chaos and then use the chaotic situation to prevail. He was able to use his celebrity status to get publicity status which he was able to do for five years with the accusation of the first black Presidency and his birthplace.

When no one ever held his feet to the fire for that public racial bigotry, he realized the sky was the limit. Why not the presidency itself? He had early learned that the show of strength was powerful, that he could bluff or bull shit his way to any deal, never to admit defeat or fault. That apparent macho male "strength" had strong appeal to much of the rural and working class males and females. He has become their "hero." When he gets insecure in the White House, he can announce a gathering to reassure his thin skin and pretend to be running for the next election.

Donald Trump is a business entrepreneur who has, apparently achieved huge wealth, enough to risk putting his name on almost everything. He is a TV celebrity who hosted a successful series. He is an outlier who has scorned most every rule or norm. He ran a political campaign he could not lose. It was a win-win gamble. Even if he lost, he would garner enormous free worldwide publicity for his name. He had such comfortable poise on the political stage he could easily bully every opponent. His capacity for grabbing headlines gained him as much publicity as all his opponents wrapped together. Not above stretching the truth, fabricating stories, three non-partisan fact-checking groups rated him as "pans on fire" lying 80% of his speeches.

The small town and rural population were his core support. Because their news sources had been mainly talk radio and Fox News, he found "dog whistle" phrases from their memory, lying Hilary, clueless Obama, brought immediate cheers. Many found him admirable, even lovable, while other recoiled in disgust. Now he is President of the United States of America, with an unknown amount of help from Russian cyber-war experts. Weave no idea where the investigation will end.

Candidate Trump found his enemy in the Washington politicians, running as an outsider who could fund his own election. He exaggerated crime, danger from the Mexican border, danger for Muslim immigrants, highly exaggerated crime rates and jobless rates. He was able to create fear, anger and distrust, constantly condemning the media, so any fact-checking reporting was disbelieved by his loyal supporters. A large portion of voters believed his pitch.

During the primary election, Trump quickly divided the country. For a large part, he evoked enthusiasm and trust, as well as fear, anger and distrust of both politicians and the media. For another large part of our country, his constant lying, bigotry, bullying and large promises brought disgust and a range of negative feelings. Mrs. Clinton won the popular vote by almost three million, but Trump won enough of the rural vote to give him the electoral vote victory. We recount the 2016 election and the first two months of Donald Trump's presidency.

Donald Trump has believed his will to win is superior to any material disadvantage. He early found his supporting philosophy in the Power of Positive Thinking by Norman Vincent Peale. It worked in negotiating Real Estate deals where big money was to be found. There he soon discovered whoever had the strongest will to win could win. He learned quickly to negotiate by force of his will, beginning with an impossible demand and when the others did not laugh and walk away, he had the upper hand. He could, with a little charm, finesse a big win even with no investment on his part.

Unfortunately Donald Trump has arrived in the Oval Office while abysmally ignorant of world affairs, incredibly uninformed in understanding the role of our country in the international world order, so ill-informed that he could repeatedly praise a brutal dictator who is our most prominent adversary. So cozy with Putin that it is strange and worrisome, particularly in the light of the Russian spying. Even though this hacking was known to help him and hurt his opposition by repeated cyberwarfare against our demarcation institutions, Trump has oddly refused to condemn this intrusion by a foreign adversary. He most reluctantly admitted facts concluded by all 17 of our intelligence agencies. This story is so convoluted and dangerous to our security that it is being reserved for a separate volume.

We briefly scan the development of his life, then his election behavior, finally, in the second part of the book, we examine his presidential behavior during the first 8-10 weeks.

This is a study of Trump's behavior BEFORE and AFTER the election. Election behaviors and Presidential behavior are observed and summarized. His management style is assessed, as well as his history of fabrication. Some 30,000 psychologists and medal health professionals have signed a letter diagnosing him as mentally unstable. There is no question that he can be delusional, frequently lying about his margin of victory, crowds size at this inaugural, and now accusing, without any evident, the previous President of wiretapping his offices. After being advised there was no evidence to support his accusation, he remained positive there would be evidence found.

It has been said often that Trump lives in a fact-free universe unlike the rest of us. His powers of self-belief are enormous and he brags how smart he is. In the latter part, we examine his executive behavior, his heedless and shameless lying, as well as the effects he is having on the more vulnerable among us.

Despite all the behaviors we find to observe and discuss here, what is stunning and worrisome is that a large part of his followers are still ready to believe him, even "love" him –at least in coal country—regardless of the courts, not the judges, not the media, not the intelligence community nor the Congress, but the now larger than life "The Donald." They are ready to believe him in preference to every other source. If any news media is critical of him, Trump declares that as "fake news," and a large number believe him.   This is why the congressional committees tasked with investigating the Russian hacking must be bipartisan.

Trump has been called a "performance artist," or "reality artist," for his ability to shape reality to his own purposes. Some even argue, pro and con, whether he is an "evil genius." Now even the conservative Wall Street Journal is joining in with editorials claiming Trump's credibility is at risk, worrying that most Americans are likely to view him as a "fake president." (WSJ editorial, March 22, 2017.

We do not attempt to offer a diagnosis for this very unique man who still stealing headlines most every day, but we do summarize that behavior which undermines trust, confounds and belittles the office of the presidency and shames our nation before the world

President Trump's problem now seems that he knows he is out of his league where he has to fake it. But he is good at faking it. "Faking big" has been his charisma. Yet, because he knows he is over his head, he is susceptible to conspiracy theories against him, highly suggestible to sounding off what whatever comes to mind, often taking his clues from the latest Suck Up Fox News , his friend Editor who publishes *The Naioinal Inquirer,* or the Shite Supremacy Bright Bart sources, mentored by Steven Banon at his side as Chief Advisor. So often has this happened that one reporter has called this "the Fox News Presidency." Others have called it the "Steve Bannon presidency."

President Trump is now so uncomfortable in the White House that he must get regular cheers from another gathering of his avid followers. We already know he seems to have no fixed principles aside from his will to power no true north unless his sense of wealth. This means, unfortunately, it seems he is essentially unhinged, with no stabilizing values outside his will to power. This means he is likely to become increasingly paranoid, subject to conspiracy theories, or he largest "whatever'" from Fox News.

On March 20, 2017, FBI Director Comey declared that there was no evidence from any of the intelligence community that supported Trump's accusation against Obama. He also confirmed an ongoing counter intelligence investigation to determine how extensive the Russian hacking was and infiltration of the Trump campaign.

A foreign power, an adversary of the free world, had effectively intervened in our electoral process. This is a most serious act of information warfare, by cyberwar against us.

Trump, by the way, at first dismissed it, called it "Nazi" and has strangely never condemned it. Possibly because he gained by it. What is unknown and terrifying is whether he or any of his staff or cooperated with the Russians. If so, this betrayal of our American institutions would make the Watergate Scandal look like kindergarten stuff. This is what is impending.

Stunning and perhaps chilling in its implications, is the blatant, shameless lying from the official POTUS twitter, from Trump, saying" "The NSA and FBI tell Congress that Russia did not influence the electoral process." The Shit-Stirrer-in-Chief had to interrupt a worrisome narrative with an alternative view of the actual facts.

Later the same day in a White House press conference, Sean Spicer, peps Secretary, was asked whether knowing now there was no evidence for Trump's claim of wiretapping from the previous President, Trump would now apologize, Spicer without pause, said "The White House supports Trump's claim."

Consider this: POTUS, that is, the President of the United States is declaring his alternative view of the actual fats to everyone: "Believe me, not your eyes and ears. "Janelle Bouie of Slate magazine describes this scene and its implications:

> ...Trump sees no advantage in accountability, no reason to honor the truth or even gesture toward its existence. Both he and his White House have made a conscious decision to destabilize public discourse, to fracture and undermine common understanding. President Trump isn't just lying to the American people; he's saying, almost openly, that the truth just doesn't matter either way. – Janelle Bouie, "Trump's Terrifying Comey Tweet, Slate, March 21, 2017

President Trump has not just been lying repeatedly, heedlessly and shamelessly. He has obtained a large portion of the voting public to accept, even embrace, his fake alternative realities, his relentless shit-stirring artistry.

Why should Trump change? He found a large number of our American people did not care about his frequent lying. They did not care he was a ruthless racial bigot toward President Obama, s many did not like Obama anyway. They did not care that he exaggerated all his claims. They did not care he was a sexual predator. And had been for years. They did not care he was married three times. They did not care he was a draft-dodger during the Vietnam War. They did not care he had thousands of claims against him for cheating workers. They did not care he did not release his tax returns. They elected him anyway. Why should he change anything?

Further, many voters did not want a woman in the White House, especially a Clinton. They loved his making fun of the smart-ass talking heads on TV news. They loved the way he would categorize politicians even our generals. They loved the way he demonstrated he didn't give a shit for political correctness. He was a bully with a bully pulpit in the campaign. When he blamed and made fun of anyone, they loved it. Trump, whether or not we like it, represents a large part of our country, ready to believe we got the short end of the stick, ready to believe the worst about others, ready to offer his celebrity status and money to be their leader.

Even this is not the whole picture, which we strive to describe later. But given this enthusiastic endorsement, why should this natural shit –stirrer change anything? His audiences only brought out the "best" in him and he could feel most at ease when with them in a kind of flow of feeling, creating an "Outsider Reality" which they cheered.

Conclusion

However we view it, Trump's candidacy in both the primary and the general and now some 50+ days of his presidency is a remarkable, even an astonishing journey. We will be talking and writing about it for years.

Certainly I am not writing for the Trump loyalists who will not accept the world of facts. We live in a flat earth society, that is, flatness is all we can see. We need to be at 35,000 feet to begin to see the curvature of the earth. We hope to offer here a vision from 35,000 feet, where curvature begins to be visible, with a larger view which can extend horizons.

Nevertheless, each view of the world, including my own, is partial, subjective and always inadequate. We can only hope these views can find resonance in others.

In this book we illustrate that candidate Trump and then President Trump deliberately stirs trouble by creating stories to amuse, distract and promote his purposes. We show he does not care about fact or truth but only his own reality and how, though the power of his will, he can gain enormous prestige, the more the better, at any cost, to promote his wealth. He was always a shit-stirrer, but he was able to evoke such fandom in his political race that he is now, shit-stirrer, *par excellence*, now striding the world, as President.

Can the reader find any indication that Trump's will to power would not remain uppermost if he had been offered hacking of his opponents emails to embarrass and cripple her favorability?

What Do We Know About Russia's

Cyber-war Attach On Our Election?

Monday, March 20, 2017 marks the day everything changed. Not only did FBI Director Comey deny President's repeated claims of wiretapping by President Obama, basically calling President Trump a liar in no uncertain terms. Comey also stated clearly for the first time that there was an ongoing investigation of Russian influence in the Trump campaign.

Director Comey was being interviewed by the House Permanent Select Committee on Intelligence, led by the Republican majority Chair and Democratic minority Chair, Adam Schiff. Representative Adam B. Schiff, Democrat of California, a former prosecutor led his committee brilliantly, through a series of questions, essentially laying out the case=as for the investigation. His word is worth quoting in their entirety: Although Representative Schiff's remarks are long; he brilliantly lays out the curious and strange coincidences that demand investigation and report to the American people.

"Is it possible that all of these events and reports are completely unrelated and nothing more than an entirely unhappy coincidence?" Mr. Schiff said. "Yes, it is possible. But it is also possible, maybe more than possible, that they are not coincidental, not disconnected and not unrelated and that the Russians use the same techniques to corrupt U.S. persons that they employed in Europe and elsewhere. We simply don't know, not yet. And we owe it to the country to find out."

"We will never know whether the Russian intervention was determinative in such a close election. Indeed, it is unknowable in a campaign in which so many small changes could have dictated a different result. More importantly, and for the purposes of our investigation, it simply does not matter. What does matter is this: the Russians successfully meddled in our democracy, and our intelligence agencies have concluded that they will do so again.

"Ours is not the first democracy to be attacked by the Russians in this way. Russian intelligence has been similarly interfering in the internal and political affairs of our European and other allies for decades. What is striking here is the degree to which the Russians were willing to undertake such an audacious and risky action against the most powerful nation on earth. That ought to be a warning to us, that if we thought that the Russians would not dare to so blatantly interfere in our affairs, we were wrong. And if we do not do our very best to understand how the Russians accomplished this unprecedented attack on our democracy and what we need to do to protect ourselves in the future, we will have only ourselves to blame.

"We know a lot about the Russian operation, about the way they amplified the damage their hacking and dumping of stolen documents was causing through the use of slick propaganda like RT, the Kremlin's media arm. But there is also a lot we do not know.

"Most important, we do not yet know whether the Russians had the help of U.S. citizens, including people associated with the Trump campaign. Many of Trump's campaign personnel, including the President himself, have ties to Russia and Russian interests. This is, of course, no crime. On the other hand, if the Trump campaign, or anybody associated with it, aided or abetted the Russians, it would not only be a serious crime, it would also represent one of the most shocking betrayals of our democracy in history.

"In Europe, where the Russians have a much longer history of political interference, they have used a variety of techniques to undermine democracy. They have employed the hacking and dumping of documents and slick propaganda as they clearly did here, but they have also used bribery, blackmail, compromising material, and financial entanglement to secure needed cooperation from individual citizens of targeted countries.

"The issue of U.S. person involvement is only one of the important matters that the Chairman and I have agreed to investigate and which is memorialized in the detailed and bipartisan scope of investigation we have signed. We will also examine whether the intelligence community's public assessment of the Russian operation is supported by the raw intelligence, whether the U.S. Government responded properly or missed the opportunity to stop this Russian attack much earlier, and whether the leak of information about Michael Flynn or others is indicative of a systemic problem. We have also reviewed whether there was any evidence to support President Trump's claim that he was wiretapped by President Obama in Trump Tower – and found no evidence whatsoever to support that slanderous accusation – and we hope that Director Comey can now put that matter permanently to rest.

"Today, most of my Democratic colleagues will be exploring with you the potential involvement of U.S. persons in the Russian attack on our democracy. It is not that we feel the other issues are not important – they are very important – but rather because this issue is least understood by the public. We realize, of course, that you may not be able to answer many of our questions in open session. You may or may not be willing to disclose even whether there is any investigation. But we hope to present to you and the public why we believe this matter is of such gravity that it demands a thorough investigation, not only by us, as we intend to do, but by the FBI as well.

"Let me give you a little preview of what I expect you will be asked by our members.

"Whether the Russian active measures campaign began as nothing more than an attempt to gather intelligence, or was always intended to be more than that, we do not know, and is one of the questions we hope to answer. But we do know this: the months of July and August 2016 appear to have been pivotal. It was at this time that the Russians began using the information they had stolen to help Donald Trump and harm Hillary Clinton. And so the question is why? What was happening in July/August of last year? And were U.S. persons involved?

"Here are some of the matters, drawn from public sources alone, since that is all we can discuss in this setting, that concern us and should concern all Americans.

"In early July, Carter Page, someone candidate Trump identified as one of his national security advisors, travels to Moscow on a trip approved by the Trump campaign. While in Moscow, he gives a speech critical of the United States and other western countries for what he believes is a hypocritical focus on democratization and efforts to fight corruption.

"According to Christopher Steele, a former British intelligence officer who is reportedly held in high regard by U.S. Intelligence, Russian sources tell him that Page has also had a secret meeting with Igor Sechin (SEH-CHIN), CEO of Russian gas giant Rosneft. Sechin is reported to be a former KGB agent and close friend of Putin's. According to Steele's Russian sources, Page is offered brokerage fees by Sechin on a deal involving a 19 percent share of the company. According to Reuters, the sale of a 19.5 percent share in Rosneft later takes place, with unknown purchasers and unknown brokerage fees.

"Also, according to Steele's Russian sources, the Trump campaign is offered documents damaging to Hillary Clinton, which the Russians would publish through an outlet that gives them deniability, like Wikileaks.

"The hacked documents would be in exchange for a Trump Administration policy that de-emphasizes Russia's invasion of Ukraine and instead focuses on criticizing NATO countries for not paying their fair share – policies which, even as recently as the President's meeting last week with Angela Merkel, have now presciently come to pass.

"In the middle of July, Paul Manafort, the Trump campaign manager and someone who was long on the payroll of Pro-Russian Ukrainian interests, attends the Republican Party convention. Carter Page, back from Moscow, also attends the convention. According to Steele, it was Manafort who chose Page to serve as a go-between for the Trump campaign and Russian interests. Ambassador Kislyak, who presides over a Russian embassy in which diplomatic personnel would later be expelled as likely spies, also attends the Republican Party convention and meets with Carter Page and additional Trump Advisors JD Gordon and Walid Phares. It was JD Gordon who approved Page's trip to Moscow.

"Ambassador Kislyak also meets with Trump campaign national security chair and now Attorney General Jeff Sessions. Sessions would later deny meeting with Russian officials during his Senate confirmation hearing.

"Just prior to the convention, the Republican Party platform is changed, removing a section that supports the provision of "lethal defensive weapons" to Ukraine, an action that would be contrary to Russian interests. Manafort categorically denies involvement by the Trump campaign in altering the platform. But the Republican Party delegate who offered the language in support of providing defensive weapons to Ukraine states that it was removed at the insistence of the Trump campaign. Later, JD Gordon admits opposing the inclusion of the provision at the time it was being debated and prior to its being removed.

"Later in July, and after the convention, the first stolen emails detrimental to Hillary Clinton appear on Wikileaks. A hacker who goes by the moniker Guccifer 2.0 claims responsibility for hacking the DNC and giving the documents to WikiLeaks. But leading private cyber security firms including CrowdStrike, Mandiant, and ThreatConnect review the evidence of the hack and conclude with high certainty that it was the work of APT28 and APT29, who were known to be Russian intelligence services. The U.S. Intelligence community also later confirms that the documents were in fact stolen by Russian intelligence and Guccifer 2.0 acted as a front. Also in late July, candidate Trump praises Wikileaks, says he loves them, and openly appeals to the Russians to hack his opponents' emails, telling them that they will be richly rewarded by the press.

"On August 8th, Roger Stone, a longtime Trump political advisor and self-proclaimed political dirty trickster, boasts in a speech that he "has communicated with Assange," and that more documents would be coming, including an "October surprise." In the middle of August, he also communicates with the Russian cutout Guccifer 2.0, and authors a Breitbart piece denying Guccifer's links to Russian intelligence.

"Then, later in August, Stone does something truly remarkable, when he predicts that John Podesta's personal emails will soon be published. "Trust me, it will soon be Podesta's time in the barrel. #Crooked Hillary."

"In the weeks that follow, Stone shows a remarkable prescience: "I have total confidence that @wikileaks and my hero Julian Assange will educate the American people soon. #Lockherup. "Payload coming," he predicts, and two days later, it does. Wikileaks releases its first batch of Podesta emails. The release of John Podesta's emails would then continue on a daily basis up to election day.

"On Election Day in November, Donald Trump wins. Donald Trump appoints one of his high profile surrogates, Michael Flynn, to be his national security advisor. Michael Flynn has been paid by the Kremlin's propaganda outfit, RT, and other Russian entities in the past. In December, Michael Flynn has a secret conversation with Ambassador Kislyak about sanctions imposed by President Obama on Russia over its hacking designed to help the Trump campaign. Michael Flynn lies about this secret conversation. The Vice President, unknowingly, then assures the country that no such conversation ever happened. The President is informed Flynn has lied, and Pence has misled the country. The President does nothing. Two weeks later, the press reveals that Flynn has lied and the President is forced to fire Mr. Flynn. The President then praises the man who lied, Flynn, and castigates the press for exposing the lie.

"Now, is it possible that the removal of the Ukraine provision from the GOP platform was a coincidence? Is it a coincidence that Jeff Sessions failed to tell the Senate about his meetings with the Russian Ambassador, not only at the convention, but a more private meeting in his office and at a time when the U.S. election was under attack by the Russians?

"Is it a coincidence that Michael Flynn would lie about a conversation he had with the same Russian Ambassador Kislyak about the most pressing issue facing both countries at the time they spoke – the U.S. imposition of sanctions over Russian hacking of our election designed to help Donald Trump? Is it a coincidence that the Russian gas company Rosneft sold a 19 percent share after former British Intelligence Officer Steele was told by Russian sources that Carter Page was offered fees on a deal of just that size? Is it a coincidence that Steele's Russian sources also affirmed that Russia had stolen documents hurtful to Secretary Clinton that it would utilize in exchange for pro-Russian policies that would later come to pass? Is it a coincidence that Roger Stone predicted that John Podesta would be the victim of a Russian hack and have his private emails published, and did so even before Mr. Podesta himself was fully aware that his private emails would be exposed?

"Is it possible that all of these events and reports are completely unrelated, and nothing more than an entirely unhappy coincidence? Yes, it is possible. But it is also possible, maybe more than possible, that they are not coincidental, not disconnected and not unrelated, and that the Russians used the same techniques to corrupt U.S. persons that they have employed in Europe and elsewhere. We simply don't know, not yet, and we owe it to the country to find out." (March 20, 2017, Congressional Hearing_

Schiff concluded: "If the Trump campaign, or anybody associated with it, aided or abetted the Russians, it would not only be a serious crime, it would also represent one of the most shocking betrayals of our democracy in history,"

Then what happened before the week of March 20 was finished is shocking. Rep. Adam Schiff announced there was now more than circumstantial evidence. The New York Times said there was the "smell of treason in the air."

Evidence is discovered by ABC news, later reported on MSNBC and NPR, that Paul Manaford, first chief strategist for Donald Trump, was paid millions of dollars to boost the agenda of Russian Premier Putin in our country. There seems no evidence that Manaford ever registered, as required by law, as a foreign agent representing another country inside our nation

Since Adam Schiff wrote this, testimony in the Senate Intel Select Committee that bother candidate and his campaign amplified the Russian influence.

How is Trump Managing His Job

As CEO of the U.S.A.?

Trump sold himself as the Ultimate Boss—the one who alone could get it done. What's happening so far?

As we complete the first 40 days of the Trump administration, multiple articles are beginning to appear questioning Trump's fitness for the office of President:

After a month in office, Donald Trump has already proved himself unable to discharge his duties. The disability isn't laziness or inattention. It expresses itself in paranoid rants, non-stop feuds carried out in public and impulsive acts that can only damage his government and himself.

Last week, at a White House press conference, the President behaved like the unhinged leader of an unstable and barely democratic republic. He rambled for nearly an hour and a half, on script and off; he flung insults at reporters; he announced that he was having fun; and he congratulated himself so many times and in such preposterous terms ("this Administration is running like a fine-tuned machine") that the White House press corps could only stare in amazement. (George Packer, *The New Yorker*, February 27, 20117)

Since md-February, the word most closely connected with Trump is "Chaos." Note below the headlines collected from some 13 different media. Each headline represents an article which can be retrieved by pasting that headline in you internet browser. :

Trump is leaving the State Department mired in <u>chaos - Salon</u>

From Oscars To Trump, <u>Chaos</u> Is The New Normal - The Daily Beast

Inside Donald Trump's White House <u>Chaos</u> - Time

Trump's <u>chaos</u> has real consequences for everyone. - Slate

Trump's constant <u>chaos</u> accomplishes nothing – The Washington Post

Does Trump's 'management by conflict' equal <u>chaos</u>? - CNN

Donald Trump Is 'Going to Continue to Create <u>Chaos</u>' - The Atlantic

<u>T's not</u> <u>chaos</u>. It's Trump's campaign strategy. – The Washington Post

<u>Chaos</u> crowns Trump's first month: Our view - USA Today

Case Study in <u>Chaos</u>: How Management Experts Grade a Trump White House – The New York Times

Trump's WH: He 'Absolutely' Wants <u>'Chaos'</u> - Newsmax

Trump's Foreign Policy <u>Chaos – New Republic</u>

On Thriving Amidst The Chaos Of Trump Era Politics – Huffington Post

Borderline <u>chaos</u>": Trump administration staffers are scared, are "in survival mode" – Salon

Donald Trump has made his vast wealth a centerpiece of his presidential campaign; he says voters can trust him because of his keen business sense. There are some problems with that strategy, however: 1) He's not quite the self-made mogul he makes himself out to be — he got a considerable head start in business thanks to his real-estate developer father. 2) His fortune may well be considerably smaller than he says it is. And 3) his business record is less sterling than he suggests. Here is a partial list of his business from one study,

1. Trump Airlines

2. Trump beverages

3. Trump: The Game

4. Trump casinos

5. Trump magazine

6. Trump Mortgage

7. Trump Steaks

8. Trump's travel site

9. Trump's telephone company

10. Trump Tower Tampa

11. Trump University

12. Trump Vodka

13. Lost future earnings from calling Mexicans rapists

Other business failures and bad judgment id detailed in this overview of Trump's business failures, "Donald Trump's 13 Biggest Business Failures" Tessa Sturt, March 15, 2016

Both the number, the range and the depth of these stories strongly suggest a substantial problem in Trumps management ability. What can we learn from those who have actually worked with him? What kind of CEO has he been?

Here is one summary of his job so far:

"Trump is selling himself to America as the king of builders, a flawless dealmaker, and masterful manager. But he isn't really any of those things," Abelson)Bloomberg News) wrote, describing not so much a builder and a buyer—at least not for a long time—but rather a landlord, a licenser, a marketer and "a golf bigwig" who "controls the teensiest details, rejects hierarchy, and picks top deputies by following his own recipe for promotion." Trump's "corporate leadership," he concluded, "is a kind of teenager's fantasy of adult office power."

The Trump Organization, longtime Trump attorney George Ross told the New York Daily News in 2004, "is a dictatorship, not a democracy."

"He's assertive, aggressive and very in your face at the same time," Trump's namesake son, Donald Trump Jr., told biographer Robert Slater for his book that came out in 2005. "He can be very scatterbrained when he talks to someone, but it's all for a purpose. He can get people confused. But he ultimately gets what he wants."

Can we summarize how he has done "on the job" since the election? Here is one summary:

He has filled a fraction of the hundreds of important Senate-confirmed jobs necessary to make the federal government work. He has signed in staged ceremonies a flurry of executive orders that have felt at times raced-out and slapdash, including the immigration travel ban that has sparked nationwide protests and panic—the revised version of which has yet to be released but will assuage, he assures, the objections of "so-called" judges.

Trump has ousted his first national security adviser in the midst of the ongoing flaring of the Russia scandal, and he has watched a potential replacement for the job beg off for personal reasons, which most likely means he didn't want to be personally subjected to the evident chaos inside the White House. In early-morning and late-night Twitter posts since his inauguration, he has attacked Nordstrom, the city of Chicago, Chuck Schumer, "low-life leakers" and "so-called angry crowds" of unsettled constituents. He has declared the press not only his "enemy" but "the enemy of the American people," dismissing coverage he doesn't like as "Fake" the way he labeled previous obstacles "Little," "Lyin'" and "Crooked." He has held a news conference in which he ranted and raved while insisting he wasn't "ranting and raving." He has had his press secretary do the same.

Trump's company, despite his grandiose portrayals of a sprawling empire, always at base was a mom-and-pop entity, and what Trump managed throughout his lengthy professional career was principally a core group of barely more than a dozen executives housed on the 26th floor of Trump Tower. Until now.

As president, Trump sits at the top of a massive bureaucracy not of his own making, a complex hierarchy designed to help him handle the most information-intensive, crisis-driven job in the world. He appears to be struggling to adapt. Hundreds of positions remain vacant, key posts have been declined by wary nominees, poorly vetted picks have withdrawn or been rejected, and the day-to-day functioning of the West Wing has become its own running news story. Trump has dismissed the accounts of turmoil as "fake news," insisting his administration is running like a fine-tuned machine. But for those who have known him, studied him and worked with him the longest, the more pressing question is whether Trump will be able to scale up. Is his well-established idiosyncratic style as a manager suited for this monumental task?

"I don't think there's anything of scale that he's had his hands on that he hasn't made a hash of," biographer Tim O'Brien said in an interview last week.

"Donald Trump sits at the top of the biggest org chart in the world. Why does he seem so uncomfortable?" Michael Kruse, **Politico,** fib 272017

Another author summarizes the White House situation in these times:

Most important, Trump remains fascinated by his ability to shatter norms. He has taken to calling on New York tabloid reporters and those from conservative outlets at his press conferences. He ordered White House press secretary Sean Spicer to conduct his first press briefing as a frothing attack dog. Bannon and Conway, campaign holdovers, often goad Trump to return to what he likes best, the sneering and jeering that draws cheers from his supporters.

If anything is clear, it is that the drama will not soon end. The past few weeks have been remarkable for many reasons, but without a clear change in correction, more tumult awaits. It took a four-star general, speaking to a military conference in Maryland, to put the full stakes in context.

"Our government continues to be in unbelievable turmoil. I hope they sort it out soon, because we're a nation at war," said Army General Tony Thomas, who commands U.S. special-operations forces. "As a commander, I'm concerned our government is as stable as possible." "Inside Donald Trump's White House Chaos," Philip Elliott, *Time* magazine, February 16, 2017.

Is it possible that the weight of the job lead to an altered, more sober, more regimented approach to management—a different Trump?

"Will he evolve?" Nobles said. "Good question."

Another former employee answered it. "I don't think he's ever going to evolve on managerial style," he said. "On policy and strategy, he may change, but he's never going to evolve in how he does things and runs things. Because that's what got him to the Oval Office." "He's A Performance Artiest pretending to be a greet manager," by Michael Kruse, **Politico,** February 28, 2017

Probably the best way to end this summary is this quote from Esquire:

> **Like it or not, sir, you're the president of the whole country. You are not merely the president of the White House, or of Sean Hannity's green room, or of whatever Caucasians-Only Valhalla lives in the minds of Steve Bannon and Stephen Miller.**

> **Sooner or later, if you want to stay in the job you have, you're going to have to talk to the people who find your presence in the White House ...well, deplorable.**

What if you'd showed up at Dulles last weekend? What if you invited a detainee family—one with two adorable children—to the White House for a chat about why what they went through, while inconvenient, was necessary to keep them safe, too. I mean, it's not like these people don't understand what living under the threat of death is like. That's why they're here in the first place.

They might even listen. But you'll never know because you're out of your element, and way over your head, and all of the lifejackets are made of bricks. "President Trump Is in Way Over His Head," Charles Pl. Pierce, *Esquire*, Feb 1, 2017

In an article "The Generals Guarding American Democracy," Patrick Granfield describes how in a White House of "unbelievable turmoil," "It has fallen to military men to keep our institutions safe." POLUTUCO Feb.25, 2-17

...Comments from Gen. Tony Thomas, commander of U.S. Special Forces, concerning recent upheaval in the White House, as well as the decision of Robert S. Hayward, a retired-three star admiral, to forgo serving as the president's national security adviser, represent an important development.

General Thomas, when asked last week at a conference in Maryland about the state of affairs in the White House, used the words "unbelievable turmoil." Turmoil is something General Thomas knows plenty about, having served as an elite Special Operations officer in Iraq and Afghanistan for much of the last 15 years. "As a commander," he said "I'm concerned our government be as stable possible."

His responsibilities commanding U.S. Special Forces also mean General Thomas knows something about how the decision-making process in the White House affects combat operations. The SEAL team leading the raid on al Qaeda operatives in Yemen late last month, which resulted in the death of Chief Petty Officer William Ryan, fell under General Thomas's command.

One of General Thomas's predecessors leading U.S. Special Forces, retired Adm. William McRaven, leveled his own critique of Donald Trump's leadership this week. McRaven, speaking at the University of Texas, where he now serves as chancellor, commented on the president's recent vilification of the media. "We must challenge this statement and this sentiment that the news media is the enemy of the American people," McRaven said, according to the Daily Texan. "This sentiment may be the greatest threat to democracy in my lifetime."

The recent presidential address to Congress on February 28 was viewed radically different by red and blue populations. His supporters gave Trump an "A' as he spoke to his base in calmer tones, hitting all the buttons they had cheered him for. Because he did not go off script within bragging and lying about his election results, the TV media fell over itself in praise.

However, to the other group, his speech was still basically a stump speech, pretending movement toward unifying of the country with no changes in his distortions. He is seen as still living in a fact-free universe. His talk contained many falsehood and misrepresentations.

Below are 12 glaring omissions, contradictions and lies Sanders spotted in Trump's address. I add one omission at the end which seems more strange and dangerous an omission than any of these 12 by Sanders on Salon:

1. Social Security and Medicare

2. Income and Wealth Inequality

3. Campaign Finance

4. Voter Suppression

5. Climate Change

6. Criminal Justice

7. Higher Education

8. "Drain the Swamp"

9. Glass-Steagall Act

10. Clean Water Rules

11. Military Spending

12. Prescription Drug Costs

(--Alexandra Rosenmann, AlTernet SalLom, March 2. 2017) Thursday, Mar 2, 2017 .

My Comment. Strange and the most glaring omission in this address was any mention of the question which haunts this administration. Why did not President Trump condemn the most serious security threat associated with his campaign? Not only has he never condemned it, but he repeatedly disparaged the intelligence report when it was presented. Why? If he wanted to put this serious threat to our democracy behind him, he would have condemned it in no uncertain terms, promised complete cooperation and transparency to his administration. This was glaringly absent.

Further, this absence fuels doubt and suspicion that there was some cooperation and possibly encouragement or complicity in the Russian hacking. Why is he still hiding, unless his personality is such that his ego cannot endure anything un-pleasant, anything which suggests a limit on his assumed popularity??

Not only was this Russian hacking, reported by 17 of our intelligence agencies, a most serious security threat and an act of cyber war, but if President Trump cannot face it and deal with it openly, then he himself becomes our most serious security threat. So far, six weeks into his administration, he shows no sign of doing so, nor any grasp of the seriousness of the issue.

I spent 30 years consult in and screening for management and leadership, literally several thousands of candidates. In his first 50 days, I do not find Trump capable of the leadership and management ability needed to lead our country.

The only roll out of a policy change by the Trump Administration so far was he Muslim ban which turned out to be disastrous. First, afar they roll out. They said did not included some types, Then it did, and then they changed again and said it did not.

In less than two weeks, Mr. Trump created upheaval at the nation's borders, alienated longtime allies, roiled markets with talk of a trade war and prompted some of the largest protests any president has faced. The Wall Street Journal bemoaned a refugee policy "so poorly explained and prepared for, that it has produced confusion and fear at airports, an immediate legal defeat, and political fury at home and abroad."

--James Stewar, *Wall Stree Journal*, February 2, 2017, " Case Study in Chaos: How Management Experts Grade a Trump White House."

When the ban was halted by a Federal Judge in Washington State, and immediately upheld, within three days a three Federal Judge Panel., the White House announced it would submit in a few days another "urgent" ban.

In the meantime, two reports from the intelligence office in the Department of Homeland Security have stated it is not citizenship from those seven countries that presents a security threat, but only the radicalization of the children of immigrants born in this country.

Voila! There is no legal basis for a ban based on citizenship from a particular Muslim country.

The first roll-out was done in haste, without betting or approval from other agencies which could have anticipated and prevented the vast disarray.

This is simply incompetence at the highest level, not restrained by appropriate leadership. The reader who wants more information can find a number of articles on this subject as they have been widely discussed.

Effective leadership demands consultation with relevant constituents, "requires an openness to being challenged, and some self-awareness and even humility to acknowledge that there are areas where other people know more than you do," ((Jeffrey Polzer in Wall Street Journal article)

Summary

The first ban rollout, I submit, is a prime example of the lack of leadership from the White House. It is appalling in the widespread confusion and personal setbacks, it has obtained.

President Trump has maintained that his administration as a finely tuned machine. He claims all the hassles are due to the media. Further he claims not only is the media the enemy of his administration, but the enemy of the American People.

This, I propose is not only scary but threatening, even ominous, portending more defensiveness, and possible circle-the-wagons conspiracy theories.

It seems as if Trump's absolute belief in his own intuition with prevalence for breaking rules, protocol and expectations will militate against creating a governing staff, properly delegated and trusted. I hope this is not so, I I fear for the direction of our country and our security.

This is not a good start for a new presidency. The President needs the hope and trust of the entire people, not just those who voted for him. The real quest now is whether he can find and implement such a vision or whether he even has one.

Trump and the Why House are calling all his troubles as due to a witch hunt by the media. If Trump was the leader fit for this position as President, he would call a press conference and say something like this:

"The Russian hacking of our electoral process was an act of cyber warfare/ the sanctions President Obama issued in response ae needed and will remain. We condemn all intrusion in our democratic processes."

"I invite a full investigation of this matter and offer my complete help and that of my staff to relieve these suspicions. WE welcome the appointment of an independent prosecutor or independent commission with legal right to subpoena.

"We and our entire staff are committed to transparency in this administration."

What is strange and worrisome is that President Trump seems to have no such incentive to honor both the presidency and our nation.

Sadly, and fearfully, I do not believe president trump can do this. He has lived for so long in the bubble of self-congratulation; he cannot endure straight feedback and the truth. His persona style is combative; he consistently overreacts and needs to imagine enemies as personal... He demonstrated much meanness, bullying and even cruelty in the political race. He has never faced the fact that his political career was built upon racial bigotry toward then President Obama. I think we can expect more drama

This, in my opinion, is the biggest Danger of all. Please note that I am not accusing Trump or his administration of anything subversive. But we have many serious questions

Why has Trump tried to tamp down any evidence of Russian hacking? Why did he summarily dismiss it? Why has he insisted repeatedly that none of his staff or team had any contact with Russian intelligence and then later blamed the media when he fired his Nation Security Advisor when he lied to the Vice president about his contacts? Why did he wait until the media found out about it tile he fired him. Why has Trump been so ready to praise Putin and repeatedly expressed positive views of Putin. Thee is new information that trump himself may have had ongoing contact with surrogates of Putin during the campaign.

Until these questions are answered, there will be a cloud of suspicion over Trump and his White House. When Trump has a record of being a shameless and relentless liar, then we cannot expect him to tell the truth about anything. At this writing, the future of our country seems to ride upon either 1) The willingness of Republicans to work with the Democratic member with bi-partisan cooperation; or 2) if this cannot work, the appointment of a special commissioner special investigator.

"Where there is smoke, there is fire,' goes the axiom. But in this case perhaps the smoke *is* the fire that must be extinguished wit required transparency, or the smoky distrust destroys the house.

What Do We Do With

A President Who Is a Liar?

To talk about Trump's lies, we really need a separate chapter. During the presidential campaign, three independent non-partisan fact-checking organizations rated Hilary's political speeches at 20% lies, but 80% for Trump. After starting his political visibility in 2011 with five years of lying about President Obama's birthplace, Trump never explained why he started this bigotry or why he ended it. In the campaign, his three main areas of lying were 1) Hilary's lying, 2) crime rate and 3) jobless rate. His lying was relentless and shameless, valuable for stroking resentment, anger, distrust and fear.

Many of us, myself included, hoped he would "pivot "after winning the election. Yet newly elected President Trump continued to live in a fact free universe, lying about voter fraud, his inaugural crowds, as well as disparaging the judiciary, the intelligence department and the press. Never was any evidence offered, nor acceptance of his error when he was challenged of his continued bigotry

Bernie Sanders puts the challenge of repeated presidential falsehoods in a post just found. Since he addressed the problem more eloquently, we start with his narration, entitled: "**What should we do if the president is a liar?**"

What should a United States senator, or any citizen, do if the president *is* a liar? Does ignoring this reality benefit the American people? Do we make a bad situation worse by disrespecting the president of the United States? Or do we have an obligation to say that he is a liar to protect America's standing in the world and people's trust in our institutions?

But how does one respond to a president who has complete disregard for reality and who makes assertions heard by billions of people around the world that have no basis in fact?

Trump said three to five million people voted illegally in the last election. This is a preposterous and dangerous allegation which intentionally opens the floodgates for an increase in voter suppression efforts. Amber Phillips herself previously wrote, "There is just no evidence of voter fraud. Why launch an investigation into something that nearly everyone in U.S. politics—save one notable exception—doesn't believe warrants an investigation?"

Trump claimed that his victory "was the biggest electoral college win since Ronald Reagan." Anyone with access to Google could see that this is factually incorrect. George H.W. Bush, Bill Clinton and Barack Obama all had bigger electoral margins of victory than Trump.

What should a United States senator, or any citizen, do if the president *is* a liar? Does ignoring this reality benefit the American people? Do we make a bad situation worse by disrespecting the president of the United States? Or do we have an obligation to say that he is a liar to protect America's standing in the world and people's trust in our institutions?

This past weekend, on March 4, President Trump reached the zenith, or "black hole" of his brazen lying. He accused former President Obama of wire-tapping his Trump offices, without the need to offer any evidence. *This is accusing President Obama of a felony without evidence.*

There are four grievance insults in this: 1) to his office, 2) to Obama, 3) to the transition process, and 4) to our government, in face of the world. This lying accusation was compounded when his Press Secretary said that the President *did not have to offer any evidence.*

This is stunning, unbelievable in presidential history. It is an affront to our nation which mocks our presidency and our country before the whole world. If accusations can be made by our President without any evidence, then we are living in a dictatorship, under a tyrant not governed by law and order. The President of the United States of America has violated his Oath of Office. *The President cannot lie, and lie repeatedly when speaking as President without violating his oath of office.*

In order to spur more discussion about this, here are a few other opinions about this:

"Trump has violated his oath to the Constitution" - ThinkProgress

"President Trump Has Already Violated His Oath Of Office" - Plunderbund; "Trump now violating Constitution" - CREW

The matter of continued presidential lying is not just urgent to a liberal Democratic Senator. We will demonstrate that concern, conversation and confrontation are widespread. Trump's lying is so extensive, unrelenting and brazen; we need the media to explore the extent. Check these websites for these titles on the internet lists

A reporter for BuzzFeed News, Mary Ann Georgantopoulos, in what seems to be an important distinction between a falsehood and a lie:

"A lie isn't just a false statement. It's a false statement whose speaker knows it's false. In these instances, the president — or his administration — has clear reason to know otherwise. Reporters are understandably cautious about using the word — some never do, because it requires speculating on what someone is thinking. The cases we call "lies" are ones where we think it's fair to make that call:

Trump is saying something that contradicts clear and widely published information that we have reason to think he's seen. This list also includes bullshit: speech that is — in its academic definition — "unconnected to a concern with the truth." –. "Here's A Running List of President Trump's Lies and Other Bullshit BuzzfeedNews: March 7, 2017

Rather than list all of these we offer here the reference clips and article titles. Pasting any of these into a browser winder will bring them up:

We Are In Crisis

We are not facing it but our country is in a constitutional crisis. President Trump is in violation of his oath of office by lying repeatedly, making accusations without offering any evidence, then saying he will appoint a committee or ask Congress to investigate to find support for his lying. We are in crises because we have a Republican congress reluctant to take any action against this president. We are in crisis because this President does not believe he needs to offer any evidence for his lying. We are in crisis because we all know that he is a relentless, shameless, liar who lives in his own fact-free universe willing to project anger and blame outwardly on others. We are in crisis because he keeps on doing this repeatedly, against Federal judges, against his intelligence departments and against the press. We are in crisis because this President believes the press is both his enemy and the enemy of the people which is the first step toward dictatorship. We are in crisis because we have a man in the Oval Office who is realizing he is not up to the job and cannot stand, literally cannot stand any criticism of his performance.

***

We are in crisis because Russia, a government, unfriendly to our values, has interfered successfully in our democratic process as reported by 17 of our intelligence agencies but President Trump disputes and disparages their work. We are in crisis because we do not know yet the extent.

We are in crisis because evidence is pointing more and more to the cooperation and actual collusion of Trump and his associates in this spying and hacking. The FBU is now investigating Russia's cyber war attack during our election.

This extent we do not yet know, but it would be treasonable and guilty of prison time for all participants. We are in crisis because as this investigation proceeds and if President Trump is guilty as seems possible, then he is likely to become more unstable than he is now

But how does one respond to a president who has complete disregard for reality and who makes assertions heard by billions of people around the world that have no basis in fact?

As we complete this book in late March, 2017, we have almost daily new examples of further lying from Trump and his administration. It seems so relentless, heedless and shameless that it can only be characterized by the term "pathological." At this point I do not think Donald Trump ever tells the truth. He makes it up as he goes. He lives totally within his own reality, creating it to fit his immense ego. What is more terrifying is that he seems to have no ability to reflect upon himself, no shame or remorse, dare say it, no guilt.

Even the conservative Wall Street Journal has now joined the chorus. "Trump's falsehoods are eroding public trust, at home and abroad." – Editorial, arch 21, 2017 7

Is Trump Mentally Unstable?

When someone is sneezing and coughing across the room, we do not need a doctor or a diagnostic label to know that person is not well and should be avoided. This is not rocket science,

When someone's behavior continually shocks normal behavior by bullying, bigotry, lying, meanness, and sexual abuse of women, we do not need a psychiatrist or a label to tell us this person is mentally unstable. The mystery in our country is how so many millions were willing to overlook repeated outrageous behavior including much lying to vote him into our highest office.

Trump was already a television personality. He had promoted himself by accusing the President of not being legal for some five years. He appealed to the voter as an outsider who could "drain the swamp," and encouraged fear, anger, judgment and even violence as appropriate. He called his opponent lying Hilary, crooked Hilary although she had not been convicted of a lying, even encouraging a "lock her up" chant.

In addition, the election was hacked by Russian intelligence to mock and embarrass both the Democratic candidate and her campaign staff. An investigation of this hacking is currently underway, even though the White House tried this week to influence it.

The results were that Donald Trump won the election on November by the highest total in electoral count. The popular vote was 2.9 million votes more than Trumps so Hilary won the popular vote.

Striking to me is that college educated Christians in my extended family network were so eager to overlook Trump's constant lying, his bullying, racial bigotry and sexual predation of women. This remains a puzzle to me. When I recently viewed a video clip of Trump's 2011 task to CPAC, when he attached the legality of President Obama concerning his birthplace, he was widely cheered by this white, mostly male group. Trump launched his political career by this bigotry for the next five years with no Republican ever confronting him. It is very possible that the bias of racism was a factor in Trump's election. He did embrace why supremacy among his fans. Now, in Steve Bannon, he has a known white supremacist as his White House advisor.

My two earlier books, Trumpism; The Shaming of our Country, and Trumpism: Stress and Resilience were attempts to express the duty to warn as seen by a psychologist.

Since mid-February, mental health professions are expressing concern: IN a letter to the New York Times, signed by 35 psychiatrists, psychologists and mental health professions, this duty to warn was expressed in these two paragraphs:

"Mr. Trump's speech and actions demonstrate an inability to tolerate views different from his own, leading to rage reactions. His words and behavior suggest a profound inability to empathize. Individuals with these traits distort reality to suit their psychological state, attacking facts and those who convey them (journalists, scientists).

"In a powerful leader, these attacks are likely to increase, as his personal myth of greatness appears to be confirmed. We believe that the grave emotional instability indicated by Mr. Trump's speech and actions makes him incapable of serving safely as president."(*New York Times*, Letter, Option, February 13, 2017)

"Appearing on MSNBC Tuesday, February 21, 2017, night, a psychologist warned that fellow doctors have a responsibility to point out that President Donald Trump exhibits clear signs of mental illness and shouldn't be trusted with the nuclear codes.

"Speaking with host Lawrence O'Donnell, Dr. John Gartner claimed, Trump is a "paranoid, psychopathic, narcissist who is divorced from reality" who will put the nation at risk.

"If we could construct a psychiatric Frankenstein monster, we could not create a leader more dangerously mentally ill than Donald Trump," Gartner began. "He is a paranoid, psychopathic, narcissist who is divorced from reality and lashes out impulsively at his imagined enemies. And this is someone, as you said, who is handling the nuclear codes."

It has long been a policy within the psychiatric community to not diagnose individuals without personally interviewing them, but Gartner — who works as a therapist in Baltimore and New York City — warned that, in the case of Trump, that should be set aside because there is ample evidence based on Trump's public utterances.

"I would argue to my colleagues that those who don't speak out are being unethical," he stated. "If we have some knowledge and understanding about the unique danger that Donald Trump presents through our psychiatric training and don't say something about it, history is not going to judge us kindly."

Appearing with Gartner, Dr. Lance Dodes also warned against not taking a hard look at Trump's mental state, which he believes disqualifies him from holding the highest office in the land.

"He lies because of his sociopathic tendencies that Dr. Gartner was talking about," Dodes suggested. "He lies in the way anybody who scams people does. He's tried to sell an idea or a product by telling you something that is untrue. There is also the kind of lie he has that in a way is more serious — that he has a loose grip on reality. We can say that because he lies about things that aren't that important."

"I think what that indicates is that he can't stand an aspect of reality that he doesn't want, so he rejects it," Dodes continued. "His grasp of reality, his attention to reality is loose. This is an extremely dangerous trait in a president. It actually makes him unqualified."

Because we have a Republican congress, with majorities in both houses, it is unlikely any impeachment can begin thee unless there is a clear and unlawful over-reach of presidential authority.

At this writing the best chance for some remedy would appear to reside in the investigation of Russian hacking which is known to involve Trump's campaign aides.

Five weeks into his presidency, it is clear Trump is continuing anger toward the FBI with disdain for the roles of agencies in his administration confirm again his self-centeredness and isolation. He has revealed gross and dangerous ignorance of not only world affairs, i.e., how this country has established an ambiance of international operation, but also of how this government works. Each day seems to bring another example of how he has no regard for democratic norms, little understanding of how government actually works, and no interest in facing this deficiency. (See "Trump is the Government," Fred Kaplan, *Slate,* February 24, 2017)

What remains stunning to those paying attention is 1) the refusal of Trump to condemn the fact of Russian hacking in our election, now being investigated by the FBI; 2) his continued criticism of our intelligence groups; and3) the recent attempts to squelch any news about the investigation, both with the FBI itself and now the key members of Congress. "Where there is smoke, there is fire," is an old axiom. It is entirely possible not only the Trump campaign team but Trump himself has been complicit, knowing and encouraging the Russian hacking. It is clear now that a special investigator will be needed to avoid tainting and hiding the facts. This would explain why Trump from the beginning was extremely critical of our intelligence findings. If he had nothing to hide, why would he be instinctively so critical?

It seems increasingly apparent that Trump 1) lives in a fact-free universe; 2) he crates fake stories" on the spur of the moment to promote his grandiosity; and 3) he needs an enemy. His recent labeling of the press as not only his enemy but the enemy of the American people is truly worrisome. By undermining trust in all our institutions, is he, possibly, setting himself up as the ultimate authority, the only source of truth?

Dodes was asked by O'Donnell (The Last Word, MSNBC) to watch and comment on a much-played clip of Trump claiming during a debate that he had lost "hundreds" of friends on 9-11. Dodes' said there were two pieces to Trump's lying: First, he lies because of his sociopathic tendencies — "He lies in the way a person scams people; he's trying to sell an idea or a product by telling you something that's not true." The other aspect of his lying was more serious — his loose grip on reality. For example, when he lies and has been told that what he said is not true, he still carries on with the lie. Dodes said that this indicates Trump cannot accept an aspect of reality and therefore rejects it, making his grasp on reality, and his attention to it, loose. "This is an extremely dangerous trait in a president," Dodes continued. "And that makes him unqualified."

Both Gartner and Dodes agreed that as far as the depth of mental illness, this is the "worst case" scenario. Gartner added, "He's just sane enough to 'pass' but is detached from reality." Gartner argued that what is *real* for the president is fluid, meaning that it's malleable. Combine this non-reality with paranoia, and being at a hand's reach of the nuclear codes is troubling. "He actually imagines he is under attack by people who are not actually attacking him," Gartner said, creating "a very dangerous combination of someone who can act on his paranoid fantasies in a way that can have catastrophic consequences."

What can we do? Be observant. Be vigilant. Write or call your elected government officials and state your concerns about Donald Trump's mental health. And hope that with the backing of 26,000 mental-health therapists in agreement that he is mentally unfit to be President of the United States

No matter whom you voted for in the election, or if you didn't vote, we the people did this — at least those of us representing an Electoral Colleges majority.

"We need to correct this threat to our ecology, our society, and our international relations soon—before it's too late." – Rosemary Sword and Philip Zimbardo, "The Elephant in the Room," *Psychology Today. February 28, 2017.*

In a *Chicago Tribune* article by Ron Grossman titled: "Is Trump's mental health a fit topic for discussion?" (March 28) he summarizes many observations with these words:

> So for the moment, let's suppose this is how my parents responded when a shrink asked why they were worried about Uncle Jerry:

> "He sits in a little room with scarcely a book, not even a newspaper, and says: 'I know more than the generals.' Jerry says he's uncovered a U.S. president's plot to sabotage himself. He thinks he can compel a foreign president to do his bidding."

> I think we know how the shrink would reply.

> "This is serious. It should not be ignored."

I do not want to place a clinical or psychiatrist label on Donald Trump. It is enough to realize that he is mentally and emotionally unstable for this job. To me, with 30 years of assessing job fitness, he is over his head both mentally and emotionally for the job as our Commander in Chief. He just doesn't have what is needed. Furthermore, his governing ability is so poor that it can be expected that his staff will be in constant turmoil, fighting among themselves for his attention and favor. This is because of a single fact: he is not trustworthy so he cannot create trust.

In the meantime, we shall need to survive and thrive despite new outrageous behavior and angry morning tweets fueled by some Fox News comment or his friendly National Inquirer.

Is Trump Affecting Our Mental Health:

American's Therapist Report

His candidacy is sowing fear, distress and anger across the country, they say. Here's what one psychologist is doing to try to stop it.

What is Donald Trump doing to Americans' mental health? It came up in the debate Sunday night, when Hillary Clinton pointed to a "Trump effect," an uptick in bullying and distress that teachers are noticing in classrooms as their students are exposed to a candidate who regularly attacks his opponents in bombastic, even threatening terms. The new revelation of Trump's crude boasts in 2005 about being able to kiss and grope women and "move on" a married woman "like a bitch" gave new fuel to the charge that his candidacy might be normalizing aggressive, disparaging talk and behavior.

This all might be another political attack, just stacked up on top of the familiar charges that Trump is a danger to national security, an impulsive and erratic personality, and indifferent to the Constitution. But thousands of therapists are worried that it's something more—and they've been saying so for months.

Over the summer, some 3,000 therapists signed a self-described manifesto declaring Trump's proclivity for scapegoating, intolerance and blatant sexism a "threat to the well-being of the people we care for" and urging others in the profession to speak out against him.

Written and circulated online by University of Minnesota psychologist William J. Doherty, the manifesto enumerated a variety of effects therapists report seeing in their patients: that Trump's combative and chaotic campaign has stoked feelings of anxiety, fear, shame and helplessness, especially in women, gay people, minority groups and nonwhite immigrants, who feel not just alienated but personally targeted by the candidate's message.

The manifesto also made a subtler point: that all the attention heaped on Trump is actually making it harder for therapists to do their jobs. Trump's campaign is legitimizing, even celebrating, a set of personal behaviors that psychotherapists work to reverse every day in their offices: "The tendency to blame 'others' in our lives for our personal fears and insecurities, and then battle these 'others,' instead of taking the healthier, more difficult path, of self-awareness and self-responsibility," as Doherty wrote. Trump also "normalizes a kind of hyper-masculinity that is antithetical to the healthy relationships that psychotherapy helps people achieve". Not to mention that his comments in the 2005 tape, Doherty says, are consistent with the behavior of a "sexual predator".

To some, the therapists' campaign might sound a little touchy-feely, a worried cry from a group whose job is to be sensitive. But their effort is also an attempt to understand something bigger about what's happening to the country.

There's good reason to believe that demagogic, authoritarian leadership has a profound effect on citizens' mental health—yet we know very little about what that effect is, Doherty says, because such repressive regimes tend to punish those who would dare to publicize findings of psychological damage. Doherty sees this moment in American politics as an important test case.

In fact, it was a recent trip to Austria, where a neo--fascist is leading in the presidential election that inspired Doherty's interest in Trump. He first thought to study what psychiatrists had done in 1930s Austria and Germany—some had collaborated with the Nazis, others remained silent—and then turned his attention to the present-day United States.

Doherty sees in Trump echoes of the cults of personality wielded by strongmen throughout history—and amplified by Trump's use of social media for self-propagandizing: appeals to fear and anger, blaming people seen as "other," humiliating opponents, fomenting distrust of the media and the political system, projecting an image of exaggerated masculinity, and ridiculing women while claiming to idealize them. For that reason, Doherty sees Trump as a threat not just to the American people but to the democratic tradition, which he believes fosters the kind of openness that is essential to the work that therapists do.

Last month, to put some research heft behind his concerns, Doherty commissioned a national poll of 1,000 voting-age Americans and found that 43 percent of the respondents—not limited to people in therapy—reported experiencing emotional distress related to Trump and his campaign.

Twenty-eight percent reported experiencing emotional distress related to Hillary Clinton's campaign. Ninety percent of those feeling emotional distress say it's worse compared with any previous election. But Trump has drawn the bulk of Doherty's attention, both because of the GOP nominee's overt aggression and because his name comes up more often in therapy sessions, Doherty says.

Trump's bombastic approach, of course, has been intoxicating and persuasive to a significant portion of the electorate. He has a kind of roguish charm, and plenty of downtrodden Americans feel energized by his message that the country needs to be made "great" and "safe" again. And certainly, not all therapists attribute their clients' anxiety to Trump or the election.

In the conservative bastion of Newport Beach, California, for instance, psychologist Michelle Matusoff, a Republican whose practice focuses on children, teens and parenting, told me she was aware of the pervasive discussion on social media about misogyny, xenophobia and racism in the presidential election. She's not a fan of Trump (especially after the release of the 2005 tape).

But she criticizes him gingerly—"He doesn't censor himself well," she recently told me, meaning he says what he really believes but he doesn't disguise it in coded language—and she calls analyses like Doherty's letter "subjective". "There's a lot of disapproving and eye-rolling among my colleagues [about Trump], but we don't notice a significant mental health impact on our clients," she says.

But Doherty is deadly serious about trying to make psychotherapists across the country aware of the psychological threat of what he calls "Trumpism," and to equip them to counter it in their practice. In his online manifesto, he urged American psychotherapists to become "citizen therapists" by actively discussing Trump with their clients and communities. I spoke to seven of those therapists, who described the effects of Trumpism they are seeing in their clients—from fear of being ostracized or stripped of legal protections they now enjoy, to suffering the terror of a childhood trauma reawakened by a candidate whose father trained him to think of himself as a "killer" and a "king". They also spoke about how Trump—with his evident lack of self-reflection and frequent scapegoating—is making it harder for them to do their jobs.

Although it's fair to assume that most of Doherty's therapists skew liberal, not all of them do. Carrie Hanson-Bradley, a therapist in Lincoln, Nebraska, says she has voted for Republican presidential candidates her whole life.

These days, she says, when her clients report increased anxiety and insecurity, they often point not just to personal troubles but to things they hear about in the news, including the Islamic State and the presidential election. Most of those clients, white males who have low- to middle-income, don't want to talk specifically about whom they're voting for. But they do express concern about "not having a candidate that represents them and their problems," explains Hanson-Bradley, who says she will not be voting for Trump. "It's really hard when your conservative values lean one way, and the candidate"—Trump—"doesn't represent that".

Some therapists say their clients are pinning their worries much more squarely on Trump himself. Fran Davis, a Boston psychologist with 30 years of experience, told me that the day after Trump's stunning primary victory on Super Tuesday, six of her seven regular clients said they felt acute anxiety just imagining that Trump could be president.

Parents talked about their distress over eruptions of hateful talk and taunting in schoolyards. A legal immigrant parent reported her child asking, "Do we have to get out of the country?" Others had uglier worries. One of Davis' patients, David Heimann, told me in an interview that Trump's racist threats against Mexicans and Muslims triggered for him fears of persecution reminiscent of his family's experience in the Holocaust.

Women have been a repeated target of Trump's, particularly of late, with his crude hot mike comments, his revived body-shaming attacks against former Miss Universe Alicia Machado and his not-so-veiled threats on Hillary Clinton's life—suggesting that Second Amendment supporters could take up arms against her, or that Clinton's bodyguards should disarm to "see what happens to her".

Those comments have touched a nerve in many women, sometimes even more alarmingly among those dealing with the post-traumatic effects of physical or sexual abuse by husbands, boyfriends or fathers.

Michelle Shauf, who works in the male-dominated high-tech and financial sectors in Atlanta, grew up with an abusive father and has recently sought therapeutic counseling. Shauf told me it depresses her to see Clinton's experience and qualifications wielded as negatives to keep her from taking on a job held only by men. Plus, Shauf, who has a 9-year-old daughter, fears that Trump's shaming of women for being "fat" or "flat-chested" can be primal injuries to adolescent girls' self-esteem.

Trump's suggestions that he could roll back civil rights gains for gay people—by appointing Supreme Court justices who would overturn same-sex marriage, for instance, and backing North Carolina's controversial bathroom law (HB2)—are similarly triggering fears in some LGBT therapy patients.

Susan Blank, Shauf's therapist in Atlanta, told me about one gay male client who was married in Vermont when same-sex marriage was first legalized there and moved back to Atlanta when Georgia recognized it. He told Blank it was similar to the movie *Jaws*: "Just when I thought it was safe to go back in the water, Trump was nominated". Margaret Howard, a licensed clinical social worker in St. Louis, said one of her lesbian clients was unnerved while traveling for work through what she described as "Trumpism areas" of the South with her same-sex partner.

To register in a hotel, they hid their relationship and pretended to be roommates. "Having to go back in the closet has come as a real shock to my younger clients," Howard told me. "They are used to acceptance".

Patrick Dougherty, a trauma therapist in the Twin Cities who is a longtime colleague of Doherty's (no relation), has found that even his mostly white heterosexual male patients—Trump's demographic sweet spot—are experiencing anger and fear as a result of Trump's campaign.

Partly it's that many of the men Dougherty treats grew up in dysfunctional families—a violent or alcoholic parent, or one who was depressed or negligent. Trump's aggressiveness is triggering for them personal childhood traumas, says Dougherty, himself a Marine veteran of the Vietnam War.

For others, Trump is contributing to a sense of "collective trauma," a blow that tears at the basic tissue of social life. The videotaped police killing of Philando Castile in Minneapolis this summer and the recent stabbing at a mall in St. Cloud already have parts of Minnesota on edge.

Trump's antagonism toward minorities and others is only making matters worse, Dougherty says: "Even here in the upper Midwest, our sense of community is disappearing". One client told Dougherty: "I work with Muslims—what's going to happen to those people?" The client added, "I'm afraid some white motherfucker is going to go down to the West Bank"—a part of Minneapolis that has a large population of Somali, mostly Muslim immigrants—"and shoot people up".

Therapists, of course, must tread lightly when it comes to discussing politics, and for some particularly vulnerable patients, the fear that Trump incites can be attractive. Mary Kelleher, a marriage and family therapist in Seattle and another signatory of Doherty's manifesto, experienced panic attacks herself just thinking about how her patients—most of whom are legal immigrants of Latin American, African or Caribbean descent—might respond to Trump's branding of immigrants as a danger.

But she was shocked to hear some of her immigrant clients say they were drawn to Trump. On reflection, she concluded, "His strongman persona represents safety to them, even if his policies could be personally destructive".

Still, Kelleher is careful not to engage in a political argument with her patients. "Their traumatization could go back decades, and that's where I would focus," rather than going directly to the subject of Trump, she explains. "Their alignment with Trump is a symptom of their trauma".

***

Trump's emergence in therapy sessions presents a powerful conflict for some therapists between their professional norms—which include not imposing their political beliefs on their clients—and what some describe as a strong, even historic sense of moral obligation to keep this candidate out of the White House. Kirsten Lind Seal, a therapist who teaches ethics at Saint Mary's University of Minnesota and signed Doherty's manifesto, assured me, "I am not going to diagnose Trump from afar, but I have an ethical obligation to make my voice heard [outside of the consulting room] about how bigotry, xenophobia, racist and sexist speech is ripping apart the fabric of our social and political life".

That's where Doherty sees his work coming in. The thousands of signatories to his open letter have become an online community that shares ideas about how to counter "Trumpism". And in August, he invited 14 of his most committed followers to brainstorm steps they can recommend to therapists in the trenches.

They discussed ideas like easing into a conversation by first asking what the Trump campaign means to the client, if the client doesn't bring up Trump on his or her own. If the answer suggests acute anxiety, then the therapist can suggest action steps, like disengaging with non-stop TV coverage of the campaign and engaging instead with friends and community. Doherty's working group also discussed how patients who feel threatened by Trump can take action as citizens rather than feeling helpless—for instance, by registering new voters—rather than turning to passive coping mechanisms, like having another glass (or bottle) of wine.

The Marine veteran therapist Dougherty, for one, is experimenting with raising the question of political stress more directly among his regular clients. "I wrote a letter about the prevalence of hate speech in the campaign, about terrorism and mass shootings, and left it in my waiting room.

I closed by saying, 'If these things are troubling you, I want to invite you to bring it into your therapy session.'" Out of 30 patients, 20 raised those concerns, and Dougherty is working to help address them.

It isn't enough to defeat Trump the candidate, some signers of Doherty's manifesto say, and that's not really the point. They believe they have to fight Trumpism—the emotional pain they say he has already caused. "There is a real and present danger for a national mental health crisis," Doherty says. "And regardless of the outcome of the election, it will continue to need our attention".

***

Gail Sheehy in consultation with Dr. Bill Doherty is the author of this article for POLITICO, published October 10, 2016, r and

First published under title: **America's Therapists Are Worried about Trump's Effect on Your Mental Health**

Reprinted here with permission. Find more about these authors at "About the Authors" on page 118.

Follow us: @politico on Twitter | Politico on Facebook

How To Avoid Cognitive Fatigue And Brain Rot

Blueprint Of 20+ Ways To Resist

Introduction. We are living in an extraordinarily stressful time. For therapists, in particular, and for many in caregiving professions, we cope with people in stress, setback and confusion. Since Donald Trump was elected, those with a history of abuse have experienced a cascade of flashbacks, hurt, fear, anxiety and a sense of dread. These rules for surviving and thriving, for wellness and resilience were first offered to a Facebook for "Citizen Therapists against Trumpism." They are updated and offered here for the general population.

RULE #: Don't catastrophize! Do not agonize or awfulize about possibilities. The reality is bad enough! Axiom: Better the devil you know than the one you don't know." Possible Lesson to be learned: what it is like to live in a Post Truth America and keep your sanity. We shall prevail. Our institutions and traditions are strong.

Let me pose a question. If we ignore the temper tantrum of a child, then should we also ignore the behavior of a mean, spiteful, insecure, vain, despicable (No diagnosis!) boy – man who seems determined to govern by his temper, to capture the attention of the world by outrageous whim? Let those who must, deal with him. We can ignore (behavior). Yes, this is an enormous challenge for our democratic traditions and even for our sanity.

RULE #2. Do not cease to be outraged. If we do, he wins by normalizing his manipulative self-centeredness. The shock and awe of outrageous behavior is strategically aimed to numb and confuse. The trick for us is to not catastrophize, wasting energy by going on about how awful stupid or dangerous his behavior is. In response to my invitation to choose your favorite word for 2017, many of you have chosen words for love, courage and resilience. Namaste! Today, "The splendor of the Light within me greets and welcomes the splendor of the Light within YOU."

Despite losing the popular vote, Trump has secured as much power as any American leader in recent history. The Republican Party controls both houses of Congress. There is a vacancy on the Supreme Court. The country is at war abroad and has been in a state of mobilization for fifteen years. This means not only that Trump will be able to move fast but also that he will become accustomed to an unusually high level of political support. He will want to maintain and increase —his ideal is the totalitarian-level popularity numbers of Vladimir Putin—and the way to achieve that is through mobilization. There will be more wars, abroad and at home.

RULE #3. Nourish your sense of giftedness and grace. Find & nurture a sanctuary place for your heart, quiet time for meditation, just breathing focus, mindfulness, yoga, centering prayer or your happy song list on your smart phone. . If you are not already doing this, consider that one percent of your waking time (c. 1000 minutes per day) is ten minutes.

Our busy hearts will sustain hope and courage when we have practiced a refuge of quiet reflection. This becomes a "think-tank for the soul," finding new perspective, and a peaceful engine for our imagination. It's like climbing stairs to the balcony where we can observe the commotion below, smile and perhaps find some laughter at ourselves.

RULE #4. PRACTICE REFRAMING. Three examples from our jail rehab program for repeat addictive offenders are: "It could be worse. My past does not determine my future." And "Fair is a county carnival that comes once each year." The more reframes you add to your list, the less you are distracted by any negativity, and the more ready you are for new situations. Reference: Resilience for the Inward Journey. A Program for Overcoming Addiction (Baute and Mercier, 2016)

In chapter 9 of 20 in my book, Trumpism: Stress and Resilience. I offer 25 examples of positive reframing (Baute, 2016). Denial is, of course, a common reframe. Happily, I discovered my first reframe at age four, my first unforgettable 'Aha moment. This has helped me cope with three major traumas, and been a template for surviving and thriving, finding resilience inch by inch. See my blog for this story, taken from, Chapter 1, Resilience of a Dream Catcher: "The Rope is Not Tied to me!"

http://paschalthestoryteller.blogspot.com/

Rule #5. *Don't make compromises.* Like Ted Cruz, who made the journey from calling Trump "utterly amoral" and a "pathological liar" to endorsing him in late September to praising his win as an "amazing victory for the American worker," Republican politicians have fallen into line. Conservative pundits who broke ranks during the campaign will return to the fold. Democrats in Congress will tend to make the case for cooperation, for the sake of getting anything done—or at least, they will say, minimizing the damage. Nongovernmental organizations, many of which are reeling at the moment, faced with a transition period in which there is no opening for their input, may grasp at chances to work with the new administration. This will be fruitless—damage cannot be minimized, much less reversed, when mobilization is the goal—but worse, it will be soul-destroying. In an autocracy, "politics as the art of the possible" becomes, in fact, utterly amoral.

Those who argue for cooperation will make the case, much as President Obama did in his speech, that cooperation is essential for the future. They will be willfully ignoring the corrupting touch of autocracy, from which the future must be fiercely protected.

Rule #6. *Remember the future*. Nothing lasts forever. Donald Trump certainly will not, and Trumpism, to the extent that it is centered on Trump's persona, will not either. Failure to imagine the future may have been one factor in the Democrats loss in this election. They offered no vision of the future to counterbalance Trump's all-too-familiar white-populist vision of an imaginary past. They had also long ignored the strange and outdated institutions of American democracy that call out for reform—like the Electoral College, which has now cost the Democratic Party two elections in which Republicans won with the minority of the popular vote. That should not be normal. But resistance—stubborn, uncompromising, outraged—should be our ongoing passion.

Rule #7. Commit to regular cardiovascular exercise. Current neuroscience states this is the best activity anyone can do for both the brain and the immune system. Gold standard is three 30 minute workouts per week, or walk vigorously 20 minutes 5 times per week. BTW, this is the best natural remedy for most all depression, anxiety and other disorders. At age 16, I lucked into a love of cross country running. I ran 5 or more miles per week for next 25 years. I had serious stress this helped with.

Since turning 75 12 years ago, I swim two miles per week. Now as a blind Veteran, my THIRD encore career mission is to demonstrate to my 900,000 Veteran brothers and sisters that this handicap is a manageable challenge. I do this by writing books on wellness, resilience and a holistic spirituality. . Browse "Paschal Baute" on kindle or Amazon.

P.S. Care now for your body and live to enjoy several encore careers, age 65 to 90! You have about 7000 waking minutes each week. Commit 100 to this CV program and be at leanest (guarantee) five percent happier. BTW, this will also help you sustain focus.

Rule #8. Eat right, prefer SLOW rather than FAST food, more veggies and fruits, preferably fresh or frozen, (they furnish healthy antioxidants, & absorb fat). Drink water. Most of us know how to eat better. Most of us do not do so. Obesity is pandemic in the USA. We eat too often for comfort. If you eat right, you will eat mindfully.

Love your body by eating healthily. Medical science now knows your gut microbiota functions as an organ system, hosting 100 trillion bacteria, of well over thousand species, all working harmoniously to digest whatever it receives, maintaining just the right mix for best digestion and flow, affecting your chemical balance, brain and mood, $2/3^{rd}$ of which is uniquely your own. BTW, your stomach will love you back when you regularly add some dark fruit like blue) berries and yogurt.

You know what you need to do to love your body more. Remember the old rule: Eat breakfast like a king, lunch like a prince and supper as a pauper. Add mindful eating to your lifestyle. PS.A little cinnamon and dark chocolate will not hurt you (smile!).

Rule #9. Remember we do not see how the world is, but how we are, through the lens and filter of all we have experienced. Little boys see the world differently than little girls. We fall in and out of love. Consider birth order: out of 29 American Astronauts, 27 were first born or eldest son. They tend to see the world through the eyes of Columbus. We are a mash-up of all that came our way. Therefore, much of this is outside awareness

This means that we need perspective, a larger view. Perspective is what therapist offer, opportunity for reframing. What we learn is many are reluctant to give up their world view. They have fringe benefits for staying stuck, like not being wrong or risking anything different.

Trump, for example, lives completely inside his own privileged reality, with blatant denial of facts, believing that attitude is more important than facts. He appealed to such distrust, anger and fear, that followers BELIEVED in him, willing to overlook repeated racial bigotry, misogyny, and shameless, relentless lying.

Those who have experienced abuse are more disturbed by his abusive meanness. It is not only because of the high office he holds but because his behavior continues. We have flashback to our abusive episodes. Since November 9, I have been reliving three abusive episodes, seeing more clearly the meanness than before. In realize one situation was more discounting that before, am glad I survived, and feel more grateful to be here. The shameless and relentless lying and bullying automatically re-energize my own haunts, inviting a new haunting of hurts long ago.

Einstein said there were two kinds of people: those who saw no miracles and those who see miracles everywhere. I choose, over and over, to be the second type, finding the awesome around every ornery, living with amazement that Mary Oliver narrates... This means learning to monitor our choosing, our choices, as well as admitting our flaws. This book is an expression of that commitment.

Is not our DNA programmed to find hope? Look how far we have come as intelligent IPhoto sapiens after 200, ooo years, each of us with 10,000 grandmothers. This is not ever to consider how long in evolution it took for our accusers toe vole to that time millions of years ago when we came due out of the trees. S Each of us is an incredible marvel and miracle. Yes, I also belie and accept the Bible as the Word of God, coming to us through fallible humans, therefore via a human envelope. As poetry, parable, story. "Concepts create idols, only wonder and awe understanding anything" Gregory of Nyssa 6thCener/

RULE #10. Take the long view. Trump is our spur for a nationwide regeneration of progressive values that keeps on giving. Already we have two generations of young people awakened to national policies and the contrast between meanness and respect. He cannot avoid meanness because he is at heart a con-artist and demagogue; e.g., he could not avoid demonizing others in his acceptance speech today.

Historical example: Before Governor Pete Wilson in California, the state was Republican, with Nixon and Reagan beginning their political careers there. Wilson and the GOP so overreached their mandate that California has been blue ever since. Trump will help turn our nation blue.

Power corrupts and absolute power corrupts absolutely (-Lord Acton). Now that Republicans have all three branches to play with, they, particularly with the arrogance of power from Trump, are bound to alienate many. It is already started happening with many form of protest.

Most people do not pay much attention to politics. Trump has changed this for millions of young people. His characteristic meanness is the spur that is already re-energizing progressive values. Besides, every good person deserves an enemy, i.e., someone to challenge their "goodness."

Trump, the Great Divider, is helping us turn our country blue. Rejoice in the challenge and the sisterhood it is creating everywhere! What an incredible opportunity to share and create change! Wow!

Rule #11. Notice how you are being manipulated by Trump, how he manipulates the news cycle; Whenever some news is not favorable to him, (e.g. the Women's March or the ex-CIA Director calling his performance at CIA on Saturday "despicable"), then he creates some news to distract so the media talks about the latest instead of the former, He has used this trick repeatedly to distract us from bad news.

Trump just did it again in having his Press Secretary rant with false claims about size of his inaugural crowd. All the media talk for the next 24 hours was on this event, not the vastness and diversity of the March OR his obscene self-congratulatory CIA performance.

Rule #12.: Never under-estimated the capacity of Donald Trump. He is where he is, in the White House, because everyone, without exception, underestimated him. He is a master manipulator and a grave danger to our democratic values, poised to do much harm.

In his speech before the CIA memorial wall, he demonstrated again, his ego-mania, using that sacred occasion to brag on his intelligence, his success, and lie about his record with the CIA and again attack the media. He has no sensed of the dignity of the office he occupies. We have much work to do. I like Bill Doherty's acronym R. A.V.E. Resistance, Advocacy, Values Engagement, We got enormous support this weekend, even from the world, let's get to work with new heart!! Amen?

Rule #13: In trying times, do not neglect regular (and new) means of maintaining a holistic balance and refreshment for your heart. These are many: exercise, meditation, music, outdoors, journaling, small group discussion, walking, cardiovascular fitness, proper diet, yoga, gardening, spiritual reading, bible verses, weekend retreat, labyrinth, establishing and following a personal "rule of life," learning to find serendipity around the corner each day, living with gratitude, wonder and awe at the mystery of our own journeys, any activity promoting mindfulness, etc. Through 28 years of the Spiritual Growth Network of Kentucky we sponsored all of these. Start local.

It is not a bad thing when we are challenged to get out of our comfort zone, to put down deeper roots, to be stretched to the maximum. One of my favorite sayings is "Every good person deserves an "enemy," that is, someone to challenge them to go farther, to "test" their goodness."

If we think we can grow in love and goodness without being tested and challenged, without conflict, we are living in delusion. Loving can never be static. Many means of re-framing and finding resilience are spelled out in my book: Trumpism: Stress and Resilience, both in print & on kindle

Rule 14. Do not become a political news junkie. Take breaks, one day, or three, or even a week. Return occasionally to one of your favorite hobbies. Tramp has been the most masterful media manipulator that history has seen. So much is still happening daily in early March, it is hard not to keep checking on the latest news. Relax. Return to your meditating and breathing exercises. Have fun, find some dark chocolate. Skip Rachel one night.

Rule #15. Keep finding hope. Many if not most of these rules have been about finding and sustaining inner hope (Including my newest book: IF I Were God)

But we can find many sources of hope outwardly. Our mutual support here, the overwhelming enthusiasm and size of the Women's March, the spontaneous protests this past weekend at our airports giving even new energy to Democrats in Congress, the courage of Acting Attorney General Sally Yates, last night, to speak truth to power, the large petition now being circulated among the State Department to protest Trump's ban. PS Rachel MSNBC evening program 9p EST, also helps me stay hopeful.

We find hope through loving, risking presence and vulnerability, sharing and giving witness. Yes?

Rule #16: *Institutions will not save you.* It took Putin a year to take over the Russian media and four years to dismantle its electoral system; the judiciary collapsed unnoticed. The capture of institutions in Turkey has been carried out even faster, by a man once celebrated as the democrat to lead Turkey into the EU. Poland has in less than a year undone half of a quarter century's accomplishments in building a constitutional democracy.

Of course, the United States has much stronger institutions than Germany did in the 1930s, or Russia does today. Both Clinton and Obama in their speeches stressed the importance and strength of these institutions. The problem, however, is that many of these institutions are enshrined in political culture rather than in law, and all of them—including the ones enshrined in law—depend on the good faith of all actors to fulfill their purpose and uphold the Constitution.

The national press is likely to be among the first institutional victims of Trumpism. There is no law that requires the presidential administration to hold daily briefings, none that guarantees media access to the White House. Many journalists may soon face a dilemma long familiar to those of us who have worked under autocracies: fall in line or forfeit access. There is no good solution (even if there is a right answer), for journalism is difficult and sometimes impossible without access to information.

The power of the investigative press—whose adherence to fact has already been severely challenged by the conspiracy-minded, lie-spinning Trump campaign—will grow weaker. The world will grow murkier. Even in the unlikely event that some mainstream media outlets decide to declare themselves in opposition to the current government, or even simply to report its abuses and failings, the president will get to frame many issues. Coverage, and thinking, will drift in a Trumpian direction, just as it did during the campaign—when, for example, the candidates argued, in essence, whether Muslim Americans bear collective responsibility for acts of terrorism or can redeem themselves by becoming the "eyes and ears" of law enforcement. Thus was xenophobia further normalized, paving the way for Trump to make good on his promises to track American Muslims and ban Muslims from entering the United States.

Rule #17. *Do not be taken in by small signs of normality.* Consider the financial markets this week, which, having tanked overnight rebounded following the Clinton and Obama speeches. Confronted with political volatility, the markets become suckers for calming rhetoric from authority figures. So do people. Panic can be neutralized by falsely reassuring words about how the world as we know it has not ended. It is a fact that the world did not end on November 8 or at any previous time in history. Yet history has seen many catastrophes, and most of them unfolded over time. That time included periods of relative calm. One of my favorite thinkers, the Jewish historian Simon Dubnow, breathed a sigh of relief in early October 1939: he had moved from Berlin to Latvia, and he wrote to his friends that he was certain that the tiny country wedged between two tyrannies would retain its sovereignty and Dubnow himself would be safe. Shortly after that, Latvia was occupied by the Soviets, then by the Germans, then by the Soviets again—but by that time Dubnow had been killed. Dubnow was well aware that he was living through a catastrophic period in history—it's just that he thought he had managed to find a pocket of normality within it.

Rule #18. Join the army of comedy. Michael Moore observes that Trump's "Achilles heel is his massively thin skin. He can't take mockery. So we all need to MOCK HIM UP! Not just the brilliant people at SNL or Colbert, Seth Myers or Samantha Bee — but YOU. Use your sense of humor and share it with people. Get them to do the same. Keep sending around the SNL links spoofing Sean Spicer, Trump and Kellyanne — there's no such thing as watching them too many times!" – Dave Urbans, *TheBlaze*, February 21, 2017.

Rule #19. You must create your own media empire. Recognize we are living in a new era where there is little difference between fact and bullshit, between reality and fake story. Because Trump recognized this, he became the greatest Master Manipulate of media in political history. He entered the political arena for self-promotion knowing he could not lose. He was bound to get enormous visibility for his Trump brand. He was so surprised to win he had neither plans nor policies on Nov ember 9.

Trump's shrewd media blitz took traditional journalism by surprise. They are barely catching up by calling Trump's lies now on the front page. If the *New York Times* announced tomorrow that Trump helped Russian hacking and would be impeached, most of the world would either not pay attention, dis believe it or not even hear about it.

This is the New World and it is media, digital media, and social media. Find media outlets, many new are digital, share their work and your own to your Facebook, Twitter, Instagram, Snapchat, and your own blog. If you don't know how to use any of those, ask any six year old. Include all your friends' family associates and digital connections. **The promulgation of Real News is now up to YOOU.**

Rule #20. Stay Engaged. It is not yet six weeks, and the White House is continuously engaged in discrediting the judiciary, the intelligence community and the press. They are trying mightily to derail any investigation by congress of an independent commission or special investigation. Where there is smoke there is fire. Power is addictive and absolute power is absolutely addictive. We have a great struggle on our hands or your heart's work, It is up to each of us to save our country from a would be tyrant.

If you thought the recent Oscars flub was a big flap, then far more drama is on the way. Nixon and the Watergate scandal will seem like kindergarten stuff. Stay tuned. For good or bad, the next months and years are going to be one of the most significant, scary, eventful periods of our history. Check out this well researched article: The New Yorker: for March 6, 2017, "Trump, Putin and the New Cold War. By Evan Osnos, David Remick and Joshua Yaffa

Extra Rule or therapists.. Accept therapy as a crazy-making profession? Do we work in such an environment? Let this barnacled, half blind octogenarian, stage 4 cancer survivor, VA "catastrophically disabled," great grandfather offer, after 50 years of listening, a thought. We listen all day, most every day, most of each day to brokenness of some sort. We live our lives inside human misery. Does this not take an enormous toll on us? Are we underestimating our need for refreshment, renewal, leisure, play-time, family time, etc.?

I started in 1961. The toll this process takes over the years is enormous. We are constantly working with the underbelly of society. I found a long loneliness in this work in which only a loving wife and family kept me sane. Journaling, regular retreats, support group, and meditation helped.

Do we need to commit more intensely to activities that can nourish and sustain our spirit? Music, meditation, journaling, etc. Check out this free app INSIGHT TIMER with over 3000 different meditations. I have been using it regularly and can recommend it highly.

Daily, hourly, we are challenged to find every type of broken person some hope, some resilience, some new vision of wellness? With the advent of this chronic abuser, serial liar, bigot, bully, insecure and reactive disparager, we have a new mountain to climb, both for ourselves and for our clients. Let us never give in but find new heart, and appreciate one another.

Is Trump (Unwittingly) Already Making America Great Again? Try These 40 Suggestions, Started By Susan Keller (*), To Find A Smile Or Two.

1. **The marital bond of millions of couples is being newly enriched**. If they are on the same side of the great political divide, they are finding new thing almost every day to talk about. If they are, unfortunately, on opposite sides, in order to avoid talking about politics, they are spurred to find new topics for sharing. :>)

2. Millions of Americans now know who their state and federal representatives are without having to google. Some even have telephone lists they are using.

3. Millions of Americans are getting more exercise. They're making and holding signs and marching every week, going places they never dreamed of going.

4. The one hundred million who did not vote are waking up to how important politics are. Since, for various reasons, they ignored their sacred duty, they are realizing, regretfully, they have no right to gripe.

5. The Postal Service is enjoying the influx cash due to stamps purchased by millions of people for letter and postcard campaigns.

6. Likewise, the pharmaceutical industry is enjoying record growth in sales of anti-depressants and anxiety control meds.

7. Millions of Americans now know how to call their elected officials and know exactly what to say to be effective.

8. Footage of town hall meetings is now, for the first time in history, entertaining.

9. Tens of millions of people are now correctly spelling words like emoluments, narcissist, fascist, misogynist, holocaust and cognitive dissonance.

10. Everyone knows more about the rise of Hitler than they did last year.

11. Ninth grade civics teachers are the new in-house heroes and love the attention.

12. Everyone knows more about legislation, branches of power and how checks and balances work.

13 Marginalized groups are experiencing an almost embarrassing surge in white allies.

14. White people in record numbers have just learned that racism is not dead.

15. White people in record numbers also finally understand that Obamacare IS the Affordable Care Act.

16. We are looking for and finding more ways to laugh. Saturday Night Live has its biggest audience ever. Stephen Colbert's "Late Night" finally gained the elusive #1 spot in late night talk shows, and Seth Meyers is finding his footing as today's Jon Stewart.

17. "Mike Pence" has donated millions of dollars to Planned Parenthood since Nov. 9th.

18. Trump has succeeded where thousands of history teachers failed – now everybody knows who Frederick Douglass was.

19. Progressives across the country are getting interested in local politics Membership in volunteer progressive organizations is exploding. This is organic, from the ground up, and so it will grow

20. Trump's travel ban protesters put $24 million into ACLU coffers in just 48 hours, enabling them to hire 200 more attorneys. Lawyers, unbelievable, are now heroes.

21. As people seek veracity in their news sources, respected news outlets are happily reporting a substantial increase in subscriptions, a boon to a struggling industry vital to our democracy. (Editor's Note: American News X (ANX) has grown by leaps and bounds since the election, for one example)

22. Live streaming court cases and congressional sessions are now as popular as the Kardashians.

23. We are having more fun with "fake news." Massive cleanup of Facebook friend list is keeping us more in touch, even renewing neglected friendships.

24. People are reading classic literature again. Sales of George Orwell's "1984" increased by 10,000% after the inauguration. (Yes, that is true. 10,000%. 9th grade Lit teachers all over the country are now rock stars.)

25. More than ever before, Americans are aware that education is important. Like, super important.

26. Millions of women, fathers, husband's friends and even children have found a new sense of solidarity and enthusiasm in the streets where no one is a stranger.

27. Muslims feel a welcome not yet experienced in many venues, welcoming at airports, etc.

28. A large portion of our population, perhaps majority feel a new sense of patriotism, of personal obligation to continue connecting, resisting, protesting, with their creativity enhanced, both red and blue.

29. A considerable part of our population believes for the first time in history that they are responsible for its outcomes.

30. Reminding ourselves of these views, we can now wake up with a secret sense of solidarity and intgerconnectiveness with millions rather than a new dread of what new stupidity will come from #45.

31. Now, more than any time in history, everyone believes that anyone can be President. Seriously, anyone. Oprah is discussing it out loud

32. Geography has become fun: Everyone now knows where Sweden is.

33. Judges and State Attorney-Generals are enjoying a new popularity.

34. We now know who is Senator Elizabeth Warren and Rosa Parks, if we did not know before.

35 Women by the gazillions are getting involved. 13,000 running foe local election this year at all levels. Countless women are feeling empowered, planning, and acting—far more than a Hilary win would have brought.

36. Through November and continuing countless mothers have forged through politics a deep and enduring emotional bond with their teen age daughters.

37. Even if we skipped civics or slept through the class, we are getting a great, ringside set into how politics works, what 'Bait and switch" does, and how fear stoked by lies works.

38. Language Arts teachers are finding almost daily newsworthy ways to teach critical thinking skills, "killing two birds with one stone."

39. In only six weeks into Trump's presidency, democracy is clearly no longer a spectator sport. Some 5,000 new volunteer groups have been established. Political engagements growing by leaps and bounds, far more than anyone could have imagined at the time of the Woman's march, January21. Celebrate this.

40. What all of this is telling us, or should tell us, is that there is no silver bullet for trumping Trump. We have a growing solidarity and mobilization across the country in regenerating our democracy. **Resistance. Advocacy. Values Engagement**. R.A.V.E. (compliments of Ed Doherty, founder of Facebook: "Citizen Therapists against Trumpism") has become an acronym for our commitment ad learning.

This list is not intended as a remedy for stupidity, malice or outrage emerging from the White House, but to provide a view from say, 30,000 feet. 2017 is an exciting time to be alive with many unexpected things happening even though some of us feel as if "we were given the wrong envelope."

Those of us who did not vote for Trump do not have to wait for months to realize we made the right decision. We are being encouraged almost daily. Can you smile at the resilience you have already learned?

This entire exercise of offering different perspectives is what psychologists call "re-framing." We believe this skill is critical to developing resilience, surviving and thriving. Short examples of re-framing are: "Well, it could be worse," "Every cloud has a silver lining," or the famous line from Shakespeare, "Tis nothing good or bad but thinking makes it so." See later chapter in this book teaching the art and skill of reframing.

"If you want to sustain a political movement over the long-term then optimism is essential." - Ruy Teixeira

*see Facebook of mischievous Susan Keller, who started this. https://www.facebook.com/susan.keller.967?fref=ufi&rc=p

My Conclusion and Challenge

I am not a lawyer but only a deeply concerned citizen, as well as one who has served my country over some 24 years, from 1948 to 1972. (Yes, I AM NOW 87.) This book seeks only to show that Donald Trump is treasonable, not that he is guilty of treason.

However, I suggest to you the evidence is strong that Donald "Trump, now President of our United States is treasonable: capable of, and likely to engage in the behavior called treason, the undermining of our democratic values by a foreign power. I suggest the evidence will soon be sufficient to warrant impeachment. Maybe not. It is possible he is entirely innocent.

Our nation has experienced an act of war, a cyber-war designed to weaken our democratic institutions, sow distrust through fake stories, and to favor one political candidate over another. The candidate who was favored by Russia won. He has often expressed admiration toward Putin the murderous dictator of Russian where opponents and journalist are regularly assassinated.

Trump condemned and made fun of the evidence of the report when it was given to him. He publically asked for hacking to hurt his political opponent, and he said he loved WikiLeaks, the agency and agent which did the stealing and revealing of emails.

Trump repeatedly lied that none of his campaign staff had any discussions with the Russians. It is now factual that at least seven had more than one conversation, some repeatedly.

Trump's denials cannot be accepted at face value. Clearly, he lives in a fact-free universe, guided by his own magical thinking of unparalleled entitlement.

I have challenged the reader to discover some aspect of Donald Trump's behavior which would offer a scruple, a caution, to deter such betrayal of our ideals. I suggest there is none. His will to power commands and controls his every moment. Ten weeks into his presidency he demonstrates reckless behavior suggesting lack of emotional stability.

In the past two weeks, hearing criticism of himself and his campaign, he demonstrated once again he cannot accept anything critical or that which might be an incentive for a personal examination. In the week of March 20, he simply lied about what was happening as has been narrated earlier. The week of March 27, hearing of the report that both he and the campaign amplified the Russian help, he replied that it was just a witch-hunt. Apparently he has never faced anything negative about himself.

Since testimony of March 30 in the Senate hearing, evidence exists that candidate Trump amplified, encouraged this outside influence from a foreign adversary. Therefore, he is beholden to it, owes it something in return. He is compromised. He is dangerous. He cannot be allowed to continue in this office, in my opinion.

This book is concerned and written with the grave urgency of a complete and non-partisan, independent investigation is required. Every American should make this a personal imperative.

The independence and integrity of our democracy and its institutions are at state. Only the independent news media, characterized by Trump as "the enemy of the people" is now plumbing the cover up. Deep investigative reporting seems found mainly in The New York Times, The Washington Post, The Wall Street Journal are reporting vital and necessary news of this huge betrayal of our democracy. Only MSNBC TV seems fully engaged in investigative depth reporting..

This book is written by an organizational psychologist who has interviewed several thousand applicants for a diversity of job positions. I am also a retired Veteran who served his country in all four branches. Being legally blind, I write this book with computer training and software provided by the Hines VA Blind Rehab Center. My other books can be found at kindle and Amazon books. Generally, he writes on themes of wellness, resilience and spirituality.

I propose there is nothing in the character, personality, background or history of Donald Trump that would enable him to say no to the offer rot help him win the presidency of the United States'

If you think or observe otherwise, I am glad to jear from you.s

What is your conclusion? What shall you do with it?

Talk to your friends. If you like this book, please leave a review at Amazon under this title. Mention it to others. As it is self-published, I have no other way, except word of mouth, to circulate it.

Allow me to close with this quote from one of my new heroes Adam Schiff: , House of Representatives: "If the Trump campaign, or anybody associated with it, aided or abetted the Russians, it would not only be a serious crime, it would also represent one of the most shocking betrayals of our democracy in history,"

Thank you for the reading. I can be reached @ paschalthestoryteller@gmail.com

Epilogue There's More

We can only see a little of the ocean,
A few miles distance from the sandy shore,
But out there – beyond,
Beyond our *eyes'* horizon,
There's more – there's more.

We can only sense a little of our mystery
Our loves and our lives—barely a core.
But out there - beyond,
Beyond our *mind's* horizon,
There's more – there's more.

There's no arrival, just the journey,
Each step awaiting thresholds galore
But in here - beyond,
Beyond our *heart's* horizon,
Still pausing - there's more.

We only glimpse a smidgen of God's love,
Blink of treasures from a mighty store,
But out there – beyond,
Beyond our *faith's* horizon,
There's more –there's more.

God's love is boundless, goodness and mercy
Flawed lovers are we – forgiveness, our chore.
But *in here* – beyond,
Beyond our *love's* horizon,
There's more - there's more.

With gifts so immense, how can we thank Thee?
By passing love on, love that doesn't keeps score.
But out there - still loving,
Beyond our *soul's* horizon,
Amazing Grace - there's more.

Mine is the morning, mine is the sunlight.
Every day's precious, fresh gift to explore.
But out there – beyond,
Beyond our *life's* horizons,
God willing, there's more.
There's more.

Advent Meditation, 2010

About the Contributors

Thanks first to my awesome life partner, **Janette,** without whose advice (and consent) and encouragement this book *could not have been written*. She read every word more than once.

Charlie Eyer, Spellbinder® Storyteller, Renaissance man of many talents, is due profound thanks for this visually impaired fellow Veteran. He has been a regular editor of most, if not all of my books. We have enjoyed much storytelling of folk fairy tales to thousands of school children. We recently completed the Kentucky chapter of Honor Flights for Veterans. He has become my dearest friend.

GAIL SHEEHY is the author of 17 books, including a biography of Hillary Clinton, hillary's choice, and a current memoir, daring: my passages. This new york times best seller is a chronicle of her trials and triumphs as a groundbreaking "girl" journalist in the 1960s, to iconic guide for women and men seeking to have it all, to one of the premier political profilers of modern times."

William Dohery, Ph.. is the founder of the Citizen Therapist Against Trumpism blog offering therapists to share concerns and get advice from one another to help handle the fears and distress of their clients. He is an educator, researcher, therapist, speaker, author, consultant, and community organizer. He is Professor and Director of the Marriage and Family Therapy Program in the Department of Family Social Science, College of Education and Human Development, at the University of Minnesota, where he is also an adjunct Professor in the Department of Family Medicine and Community Health. is an educator, researcher, therapist, speaker, author, consultant, and community organizer. He is Professor and Director of the Marriage and Family Therapy Program in the Department of Family Social Science, College of Education and

Human Development, at the University of Minnesota, where he is also an adjunct Professor in the Department of Family Medicine and Community Health.

Paschal Baute, Ed. D., storyteller, dream catcher, author, is a retired psychologist is a blind Veteran who has served his country over 24 years, from 1948-1972, in all four branches of our military. He tells this story, of surviving a troubled childhood in his memoir *Resilience of a Dream Catcher*, discovered inch by inch. His mission is to demonstrate the power of his training at Hines VA Blind Veteran Rehab Center by writing books. He now has 3-www.paschalbaute.com/resilience

Dr. Baute has some 30 years' experience of assessing mental health, emotional stability and job fitness for some 3,000 candidates, first responders, public school bus drivers, managers and executives. He is currently retired except for writing. He is married 48 years to Janette Osborne. They have three children three grandchildren and one great grandchild. He has authored 30 books with themes of wellness, resilience and an inclusive, holistic spirituality, available on kindle or Amazon.

Other Books by Dr. Paschal Baute

Available on Amazon kindle

Celtic Grace: Thin Places

Did Jesus Die for Our Sins?

Forgiveness and Transformation

God Overheard: Take Five! Daily Meditations for the Thinking Believer.

How Can I Make My Prayers Work Better?

If I Were God: A Celtic View

Me and My Shadow Self

Resilience of a Dream Catcher, A Spiritual Memoir

Secrets of Intimacy: How to Stay on the Next Pillow

Trumpism: The Shaming of Our Nation, Stress, 2016

Trump, Stress and Resilience

Union of Psychology and Spirituality

What Kind of a Perfectionist Are You?

Where Do I Find God Stories

Where Do I Find God Stories, v. 2

Win-Win Finesse, 2 volumes, with Discussion Guide

Win-Win Finesse: The Art of Dealing Positively with Negative Feelings..

Available I in print: CreateSpace and Amazon

Celtic Grace: Thin Places

Did Jesus Die for Our Sins?

Equalogue Contract: Discussion Guide for Couples

If I Were God: A Celtic View

Laughing at My Perfectionism

Lottie Mae: The Turkey Who Could Not Stop Dreaming

Resilience 29 Lessons in Coping

Resilience of a Dream Catcher

Resilience for the Inward Journey; A Program for Overcoming Addiction. Leader's Manual

Resilience for the Inward Journey; A Program for Overcoming Addiction. Participant's Workbook

Resilience: Journey of Self-Discovery

Secrets of Intimacy: How to Stay on the Next Pillow

Shit Stirrer in the Oval Office

Trumpism: The Shaming of Our Nation, Stress, 2016

Trumpism, Stress and Resilience

Trump, Chaos and esilience

Union of Psychology and Spirituality

Where Do I Find "God" Stories

Where Do I Find God Stories

Where Do I Find God Stories, volume two

Are You A Helper Or A Rescuer?

What If Stress Is At Home, An "Elephant
In The Living Room", Or The Bedroom?

www.ingramcontent.com/pod-product-compliance
Lightning Source LLC
Chambersburg PA
CBHW050412290526
45786CB00003B/1228